# POSITIVE POWER

## -ATTRACTING THE MIRACLE OF POSITIVE THINKING

## RAJ D. RAJPAL

PIONEER COMMUNICATION

# PIONEER COMMUNICATION

# BOOK SHOWCASE

## FINANCE SERIES

QUANTUM CRISIS 1-Origin of Global Financial Crises

QUANTUM CRISIS 2-The Great Financial Crisis, 2007-2009

QUANTUM CRISIS 3- Winning Investment Strategies to prosper through the crisis

QUANTUM CRISIS 4- The Great Financial Crisis 2009- 2016

## SALES AND MARKETING SERIES

QUANTUM SELLING

QUANTUM SALES MANAGEMENT

QUANTUM MARKETING

## MANAGEMENT SERIES

QUANTUM ETHICS

## SELF-IMPROVEMENT/PERSONAL MOTIVATION SERIES

QUANTUM PUBLIC SPEAKING

THE LAW OF POSITIVE THINKING -A Success Guide for teenagers & young adults

POSITIVE POWER-Attracting the Miracle of Positive Thinking

## SPIRITUALITY/NEW AGE SERIES

YOU HAVE IT ALL NOW: Your Life is truly yours to discover & enjoy

UNCONDITIONAL LOVE

BEYOND THE MIND

TOWARDS THE UNKNOWN

# POSITIVE POWER

## -ATTRACTING THE MIRACLE OF POSITIVE THINKING

## RAJ D. RAJPAL

B.Sc. (Honors), D.A.P.R., D.M., D.C.S., D.P.S., M.B.A. (Ohio)

Sales Coach and Public Speaker

Canadian National Quality Award Winner

Trainer, Bob Proctor Basic Program, Canada

Magna cum Laude, MBA Program, Ohio, U.S.A.

Sales Trainer, Counselor Selling Program, U.S.A.

Trophy Winner, Public Speaking, Indo-American Society

Provisional Applicant, Million Dollar Round Table, U.S.A.

Diploma, Graduate Advertising & Public Relations Program.

Trainer, Bob Proctor Advanced Motivation Series Program, Canada

Uni Lever Gold Medal Recipient-Graduate Marketing Management Program

PIONEER COMMUNICATION

PUBLISHER:

PIONEER COMMUNICATION, CANADA

Orders for additional books can be placed directly at:
Pioneercommunication1@yahoo.com

(Sales Discounts on multiple copy orders)

National Library of Canada

Rajpal Raj D., 1951-

Positive Power/Raj D. Rajpal

ISBN: 978-0978355098

Copyright 2016 Raj D. Rajpal  ALL RIGHTS RESERVED

This book is dedicated to the emotional, intellectual and spiritual growth of adults worldwide.

May the new found glimpse of truth and understanding create a wave of Light, which shines brightly and eliminates all your worry and lacuna of External Life Result. And may this Light shine clearly as a solution, which aids in the accomplishment of your goals, dreams and desires.

And most importantly, may you be able to generate an everlasting and abundant source of Happiness created through attraction of the miracle of Positive Thinking.

# TABLE OF CONTENTS

# SECTION 1

## THE UNIVERSAL LAWS OF POSITIVISM

CHAPTER 3

Understanding the Law of Attraction

CHAPTER 4

Applying the Law of Attraction through Positive Thinking

CHAPTER 5

Understanding the Law of Success

CHAPTER 6

The Law of Success in relationship with Positive Thinking

CHAPTER 7

Understanding the Law of Sub-conscious Power (a.k.a. the Power of the Sub-Conscious Mind)

CHAPTER 8

The Sub-Conscious Mind and the Power of Positive Thought

CHAPTER 9

Understanding the Law of Psycho-Cybernetics

# CHAPTER 10

Applying Principles of Psycho-Cybernetics to Positive Thinking

# SECTION 2

## THE BASICS

CHAPTER 11

Why you should think and act positively

CHAPTER 12

Decide what you want

CHAPTER 13

Believe your goal is achievable

CHAPTER 14

Believe in yourself

CHAPTER 15

Have a Positive Mental Attitude

CHAPTER 16

Be an Inverse Paranoid

CHAPTER 17

Take action and keep score

# SECTION 3

## POSITIVE THINKING & RELATIONSHIPS

Positivism and goal setting

Positivism and a plan of action

Positivism and goal setting

Positivism and your life strategy/portfolio

Positivism and Self-Motivation

Positivism and Self-Image

Positivism and Self-Concept

Positivism and the Law of Attraction

Positivism and the Energy of Desire

Positivism and good relationships

Positivism and good health

Positivism and longevity and a disease free life Positivism and wealth creation

Positivism and Stress Management

Positivism and Entrepreneurship

Positivism and Self-Confidence

Positivism and Time Management

Positivism and the Art of Allowing

Positivism and Parenting

Positivism and the power of the Master Mind

Positivism and the Law of Karma

Positivism and the Law of Prosperity

# SECTION 4

## APPLICATION OF POSITIVE PRINCIPLES IN CREATING HAPPINESS

CHAPTER 19

POSITIVISM AND HAPPINESS

Definition of Happiness

Relationship between Positive Thinking and Happiness

Happiness and Negative Thinking-An inherent contradiction


CHAPTER 20

NEGATION OF POSITIVISM

"Never ending desire for more stuff."

Positivism and giving up grudges


CHAPTER 21

POSITIVISM, HAPPINESS AND KARMA


CHAPTER 22

THE SHADOW OF FEAR-THE ANTITHESIS OF HAPPINESS


CHAPTER 23

POSITIVISM AND LACK OF WORRY

# INTRODUCTION

Positive thinking forms the wellspring of all human motivation. And the reception of positive thinking has been something taken for granted by humans. Let me explain what I mean by this statement: *the message here is that we all seem to be exposed to positive thinking at some time or another in our Life and we, in most instances, accept the concept of positive thinking*. Personal development and positive thinking gurus have, through the medium of radio, television and press expounded the benefits of positive thinking. However this teaching has in most cases become only an addition to our already existing memory bank. These valuable teachings now only represent a half-baked truth, which while being accepted, is rarely acted upon at a deeper level. When you ask a person on the street what he makes of the idea of positive thinking, his "take on the matter" is that he hears the message that there exists a possibility of achieving happiness and success by being positive------ very rarely have I encountered an individual who takes this learning serious enough to initiate movement to the next step of experience. To engage in such learning involves an active exploration into all the ramifications of Positive Thinking and its value in the Life transformation process.

And this is what I have tried to do through this book. I have worked hard in presenting ideas, which will necessarily spark a deeper understanding of the miracle of positive thinking. This wonderful miracle does not exist in a vacuum but is like Life, mysteriously and coherently intermingled with human relationship. To truly understand Positive Thinking, one must see all its interlinked weaving's, which are governed by the Natural Laws like the Law of Attraction, the Law of Psycho-Cybernetics, The Law of the Subconscious Mind and the Law of Success.

One must further delve into the nature of human relationship and see how such relationships are influenced by the use/disuse of positive thinking. In this relating process, a person has two choices and only two choices, which is either to be positive or to express himself negatively. Every action has an equal and opposite reaction. And this Newtonian law applies so clearly to your choice of being either positive or negative. The resultant reaction to this choice is self-evident. A positive personality is a sparkling one and creates an air of trust, love and understanding attracting others to his cause and way of Life.

A negative personality, on the other hand, is one which draws negative forces like anger, frustration, stress and hatred and results in the creation of a social environment characterizing such person as offensive, abusive and not worthy of time and attention. The real question here is: "We all want to be loved and respected and trusted, but knowing the result accompanying the choice between good (positive) and evil (negative), why do we, at so many points in our Life, express ourselves through negativism?"

I challenge every reader to take his Life to the next level----- to open himself to a Life blessed with much grace and happiness. I also challenge every reader to use these principles and relationship strands to better his Life. It is said that we attract both misery and happiness into our Life------ a normal day and a lifetime are both filled with times of sorrow and happiness. It is your challenge to make every moment and second of your Life happy and fulfilling and if this is not possible for you, at least an attempt by you to create a Life, which is filled with much happiness and enthusiasm and accompanied with a detached attitude towards your pain and stress.


It is the author's firm prayer that he can, in whatever small way, assist every reader learn all the fundamental principles of Positive Thinking as these apply to the reader's own unique and special Life. The author also prays that a person can transform his Life to a more elevated sense of consciousness in which all good things happen. Do not forget you control the mental and emotional space within; accept pain and stress and you become that pain and suffering----- refuse to be subdued and live a life of positivism and passion and such Life will only lead you to increased health, vitality and success.


This book can play a role in your personal growth and development, otherwise what is the purpose of this book or any other book on personal development??????? But, as the old saying goes, "it takes two hands to clap." Therefore, a curious sense of attentiveness on your part accompanied with a childlike curiosity and an open heart are all required in this journey to better yourself. Please try to listen to the message contained in this book with an open mind, while reserving judgment to the end.

Learn to make a quantum change in the quality of your Thought------ and your Life will mirror that Positivism---- it will transform itself into a Life blessed with more success, happiness and a sense of ease as you arrive in a better station of Life. You will be more loved and respected. And your new found trust will lead to better relationships, which will in turn lead to more success in all aspects of your Being, whether this be physical, emotional, mental and/or Spiritual. And is this not the real Purpose of Life----- to be happy and to make others happy through superlative service and the employment of Positive Thinking?????

# PREFACE

## BOOK STRUCTURE, DESIGN AND OBJECTIVES

This book is designed to operate and express ideas and feelings within a natural free-flowing structure. The main presentation of this book starts with an understanding of the philosophy and psychology behind positive thinking.

THE FIRST SECTION starts with a discussion of the **four powerful Universal Laws, which influence everything in our Life:**

The Law of Attraction.

The Law of the Sub-Conscious Mind.

The Law of Success and

The Law of Psycho-Cybernetics.

An understanding of these four laws is crucial before one begins a study into Positive Thinking.

THE SECOND SECTION deals with the basic concepts and principles of positive thinking and is an introduction to the subject area.

THE THIRD SECTION discusses the principles of Positive Thinking as they apply in different Life situations. This section deals with how Positive Thinking relates to specific aspects of your different Life Relationships.

The FOURTH SECTION of the book then attempts to explain the relationship between Positive Thinking and Happiness. It explains that while happiness and self-contentment is sought by so many, that it it, at best, remains an elusive goal to most humans.

The objectives of this book are to create a smooth, simple platform for the study of important concepts of Positive Thinking. After this, the book tries to show you how to apply these concepts and principles in your varying relationships at Work, Home and Play. **The net intended result is more balance, peace and happiness in your Life** as you strive to improve and perfect your relationships with all the significant players in your Life. And Success inevitably follows the understanding and implementation of Positive Thinking in your relationships with all the important people in your Life.

Life is all about sharing and in the process, serving others. May this book in its presentation assist you in achieving all your Life goals, whether these be personal, business, or Life oriented. And above all, may it be a true and shining light, which allows you to be balanced, happy and content as you weather all of Life's storms. May you make lemonade when Life hands you a lemon and may every journey be filled with wisdom and new beneficial experience.

# CHAPTER 1

## PHILOSOPHY BEHIND POSITIVE THINKING

Life is a constant challenge and Man tries to meet or exceed every challenge. Challenges are numerous and too many to quantify. Some of the significant challenges facing Mankind are the struggle to physically survive, the challenge of finding enough food, the need of locating suitable shelter and the challenge to bond and mate with another. Equally significant is the challenge of finding a way where we can all live together in Peace and Harmony, setting up standards and rules, which govern our actions towards each other in both civil and non-democratic societies.

The way Man has historically faced up to his challenges and responsibilities collectively is a disaster. Through two bloody World Wars and constant battles and skirmishes in between and afterward, it appears that the prime objective of primitive, medieval and modern society is the desire to dominate the weaker for material, physical and political gain. In the process, we have destroyed the fabric of Humanity and created numerous ills, resulting in poor outcomes for each other. Global warming, a degradation of the human environment, corruption and violence have caused their toll on Man.

Given this difficult set of circumstance, one needs to identify factors which can create and sustain happiness through peaceful and intelligent cooperation with each other. And this where Positive Thinking comes in. It is two things: firstly, it is a mindset, which governs the way we see ourselves. Secondly it is an attitude towards others, which helps us cooperate and coexist non-violently. It is a realization that there is enough for everyone and that the real competition is within oneself and not with others.

Positive thinking can be imagined as a gateway, a method and way of Life, which can bring Harmony and Peace in all relationships. For most of Mankind, it is a veritable challenge to think positively all the time, since a host of circumstances around us negate the very meaning of Life and Positivity. It seems unsurprising then, that the very few who stay positive most of the time are able to attract their wishes and dreams more than the general level of populace who are controlled more by their emotions and negativity when faced with severe economic and environmental challenges.

The meaning of Positivity has also changed with Time and Economic circumstance. In older religions from the East, a reverence and faith to a chosen God seemed to be an appropriate way of indicating a spirit of humility and positivism. And in many inexplicable ways, it was. Cultivation of faith and humility have always been essential ingredients of positivism.

As the West was conquered in the 18th century, new civilizations which were hardly a few hundred years old had to face a new set of challenges----- some of these challenges pertained to a struggle to control and vanquish the indigenous population (a cruel, senseless act at the best), the challenge to develop agricultural uses of land and a whole host of economic, social and religious issues as the new population adjusted to a strange and foreign environment. In the early twentieth century several notable North American philosophers and positive thinkers advanced the doctrine of Positive Thinking. Use of Positive Thinking appeared to these New Age thinkers to be the best and only way to withstand, overcome and stay on top of all the negativism accompanying cruel acts of people as they strive to live in a new land. Slowly, but surely, the concepts of Positive Thinking took root. Some of the predominant early advocates were Napoleon Hill, Scovill and a host of other prominent and original Western thinkers.

As the societies of the West got more developed, new challenges arose like societal inequality and unfair distribution of wealth. Also for the first time, new problems like unemployment, high cost of living, broken marriages and delinquent teenagers and increasing violence dominated the landscape. There was an urgent need for a new way of thinking, for a new way of Life and most important a new way of relating with each other. It is in this role that Positive Thinking has made the greatest contribution to Mankind. The promise that it is open to each and every human being, irrespective of his educational attainment, his IQ or family wealth situation, the fact that it can be molded to the dreams and wishes of the poor and rich alike and that it creates an equalized economic playing field for all constitutes its most notable achievement to Mankind.

The other great role of Positive Thinking is in its attempt to uplift Mankind by exhorting Man to look deep within himself for answers to Life's mystery. From times immemorial, the basic question, which encompasses and pre-empts all other Spiritual questions is the one which asks: "Who am I?" Ramana Maharishi, one of the most notable sages of India has often said that before you ask or do anything else spiritually that you first take the time to seriously ponder the meaning behind this question and only after you answer this question satisfactorily to yourself can you proceed meaningfully towards a spiritual journey.

Positive thinking is a "diamond in the rough". It asks you to get into yourself to understand what you are all about---- it challenges you to understand your relationship with the Universal Energy and it provides a broad prescription of strategies to assist you live a more wholesome, meaningful Life where you can serve others while achieving your own personal Goals. In that sense, Positive Thinking plays an important role in the march of both humanity and Nations.

A philosophical grasp of the content and application of Positive Thinking will assist you in becoming a more rounded person; it will attract within you the qualities to bring about abundance, peace and happiness in your Life; it will also be the wellspring, which will draw Success in every field of desired endeavor, whether this be achievement of a personal goal or your dream to contribute positively to Society and Mankind.

# CHAPTER 2

## PSYCHOLOGY BEHIND POSITIVE THINKING

As man grows and evolves in his surrounding and circumstance, he needs to find meaning in everything he does. Now his cerebral powers are developed both physically and genetically and Life is not just about hunting and mating. Man now searches for aesthetic pleasures but more importantly tries to find a meaning to his Life.

A real challenge now is to understand his relationships with the environment, his relationship with his thoughts and feelings and his association with his loved ones. As he strives to excel in his work, he is confounded by a series of setbacks and failures. Accompanying such setbacks is the accompaniment of much resentment, anger and depression. It now appears to him that Life is all about *"hitting the mark,"* in addition to working hard----he sometimes becomes desperate due to his inability to attract what he wishes within a short period of time.

Societies, cultures and individuals have searched for an easy way to express themselves with a view to attracting instant Success in Life. As Societies evolve, there has been an awarding of more freedom to Man. He is free to choose his avocation and his mate------he also has the choice now to live Life on his own terms. What creates a real challenge is the obstacles he must face in his constant challenge to feed himself, in his search towards finding and holding a mate, in his acquisition of chosen pleasures and his quest towards attainment of professional success(while earning enough to satisfy his needs, wants and special desires). Accompanying this setback to success, which happens sporadically, is the onset of pain, struggle and sometimes a sense of despondence.

New Age thinkers in the West (dating back to almost two hundred years back) have tried to find a solution to this dilemma. They have researched intensively to determine why some people get everything they desire and others struggle their entire lifetime and do not get very far in fulfilling their goals and desires. Great minds like Napoleon Hill, Dale Carnegie, Scovill and Gerry Hicks have come up with theories on Positive Thinking and the Law of Attraction. These are really only theories till you actually use them and find out if they work in your life.

The Psychology of Positive Thinking involves creating a fresh mental and emotional look towards Life. This Psychology teaches you how to intelligently comprehend your thoughts and feelings, it guides you in gauging where you are at in your Life with respect to your goals and desires. But most importantly, Positive Thinking teaches you how to project your desires forward to achieve your goals easily.

Positive Thinking has now taken on the attributes of a scientific method of expression. There are very specific scientific ways to growing personally using this Psychology of Positive Thinking. There is also the Law of Attraction which works in companionship status with the Law of Positive thinking to help you accomplish what you need. This newly developed Psychology aids you in determining and executing actions linked to future Success like goal setting, visualization, personality analysis, measurement of goal achievement among other things. Positive thinking psychology works hand-in-hand with personal motivation objectives, which assist in building self-esteem while projecting forth and crystallizing your stated desires. Most importantly again, positive thinking psychology leads to a gateway which opens into an expression of the power of intent----- a process where you emotionally allow yourself to receive the fruits of your desires. Through the allowing process, you consciously allow the desired changes to manifest themselves in your Life, before they have actually crystallized in your present moment. If you believe in your dreams coming true and project in advance mode that you have already achieved what you want, then it is that much easier for the dream to come true.

The psychology of positive thinking is a proven system of Life and if properly utilized is guaranteed to change your Life around and give you a simple and easy way to get what you want. Work hard at making your dreams come true. But do not forget to employ the entire Psychology and its companion Laws to work for you in unison to assist you in reaching your goals. One needs to employ all the Companion Laws like the Universal Laws of Attraction, The Law of Power of the Sub-Conscious Mind, Law of Psycho-Cybernetics and Law of Success-------in addition one must apply all the personal motivation principles including the power of visualization, the technique and art of goal setting, goal monitoring and the application of the power of intent to make results materialize quickly in your Life.

*The Psychology of Positive Thinking is a must for the unfoldment of your Success and Happiness.*

# CHAPTER 3

## UNDERSTANDING THE LAW OF ATTRACTION

Everything starts and ends with the Law of Attraction. So, before we start our study of Positive Thinking, we must first understand the Theory and Practice of the Law of Attraction. Let us first move into the Theory of the Law of Attraction. This Theory postulates that the Mind is the most powerful instrument under our control and the thoughts projected by the Mind represent the source of its Power over all our future results. Thought and its associated vibrations create a magic "halo effect"----- a real magnetic wave, which can alter your Life for the better or worse. This Law further states that if you dwell on any particular thought in an intensive focused mode, that this Thought will attract its counterpart from the external environment. So, if you want to get rich, and you constantly dwell on that thought, the power of this intense focus will draw the riches of the world to you. At first sight, this sounds too good to be true. A Man's rational mind will probably not allow him to accept this premise easily. As many of us are brought up in a rational and Western cultural environment, which teaches us to believe in something only after we see it, an ordinary person immediately rejects this theory of results magically arising by simply focusing on what one wants-----this misunderstanding and non-comprehension means that an average person loses out on one of the most important Natural laws of the Universe. In order to correct this misconception a person needs to reverse and reject his normal rational thought process. This person now makes a fundamental shift in his way of viewing his Life and the results which flow from his actions. When he goes from saying, "I will believe it when I see it,"to a state of Mind which says "I will believe the fact that I already possess what I wish and as a result of this belief such result will automatically manifest itself in my future." Now this Mind has become a Super Mind and is ready for a quantum shift in consciousness, which creates a new and better result for him.

The Practice of the Law of Attraction, assuming that you have either accepted this theory outlined above or are at the very least open-minded enough to experiment with this novel Law, results in you creating results, which are compatible with your mindset. The intensity and speed of the result is really determined by how passionately you want something and how well you apply this Law of Attraction. Let me elaborate: if you are very passionate about your belief surrounding a particular thought, if you fully and completely allow that new experience to happen in your Life and you totally accept it will become a reality, then you will attract it quickly.

This Law of Attraction works on all levels of your existence: the physical, the mental, the emotional and spiritual level. The Principle behind the Law of Attraction is that there are distinct physical and non-physical laws, which affect humans. We are already familiar with the physical Laws of gravity and energy among other things. But we do not pay the same level of attention to Non-Physical Laws. What is a non-physical law? It is a law which is difficult to quantify and test and deals with the relationship between Man and the Energy around him. Many people falsely believe that all results created are due to effort and knowledge only. There is a third dimension and this is the dimension of Energy Spirit. What this translates to is the fact that two men with almost the same level of intelligence, knowledge and effort create two different Life results; this difference in result may be attributed to the presence of an ethereal, magnetic third factor, which then creates the difference in result between these two equally matched men. This element of difference belongs to the non-physical world, to the world where energy in the environment is influenced by Man's desire, passion and open-mindedness to a desired result. The non-physical realm has attracted many New Age Philosophers, who strive to explain the reasons behind extraordinary success of some political, business and social leaders. These philosophers also point out that the same non-physical forces can go to work for a common Man thereby guaranteeing him the same level of success as such leaders. This now becomes a powerful motivating force for the common man to rise above his common denominator.

The Law of Attraction refers particularly to an understanding of these non-physical laws. These determine the mysterious way in which the Energy around you is attracted to your wishes and dreams. This is initially a difficult concept to grasp but it deals with the attraction of energy directly into the fulfillment of your desire. How such law of attraction works is not known in specific detail. But it is known quite universally that those who have a specific goal, attach desire to such goal and work conscientiously towards reaching their dream by moving positively in their chosen direction, always get what they want. Some achieve their goal faster and others take longer but all of them get what they want. The Universe provides the energy critical for the fulfillment of their goals.

The next chapter will deal with how Positive Thinking works in making the Law of Attraction a reality and success in your Life. For this chapter, it is suffice to say that the Law of Attraction is a real and powerful Non-Physical Law of the Universe and for those who dare enough to experiment and work with this law, the fruits of such effort are limitless. If you want to become successful and achieve your wishes, goals and dreams nothing will get you there faster than employment and application of the powerful Law of Attraction.

.

# CHAPTER 4

## APPLYING THE LAW OF ATTRACTION THROUGH POSITIVE THINKING

The Law of Attraction encourages young and old alike to clarify what they truly desire out of their Life. It also asks them to prioritize their goals and desires. Further it challenges them to go after their desires with a spirit of Allowing. What is this spirit of Allowing? It is the cultivation of a deep, emotional space within you, which means you giving yourself the permission to attain and fulfill any desire you wish for. And that Allowing process then assists in the speedy manifestation of your desire and goal. The Law of Allowing is also referred to as the Law of Intention----- a process where you beforehand intend to attract the results you strive for in your Life.

As one embarks on this journey towards self-fulfillment, one encounters challenges and obstacles in the way. At times in your Life, you try very hard to get what you want, only to have someone slap rejection on your face. The rejections one faces on the Road to Success are numerous and require a special state of Mind This is where positive thinking comes to your rescue. Positive thinking allows you to believe in yourself and in your dreams. It gives you the strength to forge ahead not abandoning your goal or your actions and efforts towards it. Positive thinking when combined with the Law of Attraction allows you to stay focused and supports your faith in this Law of attraction. Through positive thinking you support the entire concept of Law of Attraction, which says again and again that where the Mind chooses to focus its thoughts is where Life draws itself into the person. So, if you choose positive thoughts with complete belief in attainment of your goals, then surely that must pass. If, however, you choose negative thoughts and do not expect to reach your goal then that is what you will achieve-------- a lifetime of bitterness, anger, desperation and depression as you keep missing one goal after another.

The promise of positive thinking is open to all, rich or poor, young or old. It is indeed an equalizer which cuts through all age, economic and education barriers. Positive power accompanied by the Law of Attraction is a never relenting force which draws all the necessary ingredients from the environment to make you that much more successful in less time and with superlative result.

# CHAPTER 5

## UNDERSTANDING THE LAW OF SUCCESS

The Law of Success was first propounded by the famous motivation and success guru, Napoleon Hill. This Law found expression in the form of a course designed by Napoleon Hill in 1928. Napoleon spent several years designing this course by consulting several successful businessmen, politicians and social workers in the US. Discussions, meetings and advice from such leaders found themselves as valuable course material for this Law. This Law of Success is a natural Universal Law. Before we can even touch on the subject of Positive Thinking, we need to understand and appreciate this Law.

The Law of Success presents fifteen basic principles, which when utilized can assist any person to elevate himself from a position of average or mediocre performance to one of super-success. These laws are as relevant to our way of Life today as they were back in 1928. Below is reproduced, in the Master's hand itself, the 15 universal principles creating and maintaining Success. I take great pleasure now in reproducing an excerpt from the original book, "Law of Success" authored by Napoleon Hill:

I.      A DEFINITE CHIEF AIM will teach you how to save the wasted effort, which the majority of people expend in trying to find their lifework. This lesson will show you how to do away forever with aimlessness and fix your heart and hand upon some definite, well conceived purpose as a life-work.

II.      SELF-CONFIDENCE will help you master the six basic fears with which every person is cursed-the fear of Poverty, the fear of Ill-Health, the fear of Old Age, the fear of Criticism, the fear of Loss of Love of Someone and the fear of Death. It will teach you the difference between egotism and real self-confidence, which is based upon definite, usable knowledge.

III.      HABIT OF SAVING will teach you how to distribute your income systematically so that a definite percentage of it will steadily accumulate, thus forming one of the greatest known sources of personal power. No one may succeed in life without saving money. There is no exception to this rule, and no one may escape it.

IV.      INITIATIVE AND LEADERSHIP will show you how to become a leader instead of a follower in your chosen field of endeavor. It will develop in you the instinct for leadership which will cause you gradually to gravitate to the top in all undertakings in which you participate.

V.     IMAGINATION will stimulate your mind so that you will conceive new ideas and develop new plans which will help you in attaining the object of your Definite Chief Aim. This lesson will teach you how to "build new houses out of old stones," so to speak. It will show you how to create new ideas out of old, well known concepts, and how to put old ideas to new uses. This one lesson, alone, is

the equivalent of a very practical course in salesmanship, and it is sure to prove a veritable gold mine of knowledge to the person who is in earnest.

VI.     ENTHUSIASM will enable you to "saturate" all with whom you come in contact with interest in you and in your ideas. Enthusiasm is the foundation of a Pleasing Personality, and you must have such a personality in order to influence others to co-operate with you.

VII.    SELF-CONTROL is the "balance wheel" with which you control your enthusiasm and direct it where you wish it to carry you. This lesson will teach you, in a most practical manner, to become "the master of your fate, the Captain of your Soul."

VIII.   THE HABIT OF DOING MORE THAN PAID FOR is one of the most important lessons of the Law of Success course. It will teach you how to take advantage of the Law of Increasing Returns, which will eventually insure you a return in money far out of proportion to the service you render. No one may become a real leader in any walk of life without practicing the habit of doing more work and better work than that for which he is paid.

IX.     PLEASING PERSONALITY is the "fulcrum" on which you must place the "crow-bar" of your efforts, and when so placed, with intelligence, it will enable you to remove mountains of obstacles. This one lesson, alone, has made scores of Master Salesmen. It has developed leaders over night. It will teach you how to transform your personality so that you may adapt yourself to any environment, or to any other personality, in such a manner that you may easily dominate.

X.      ACCURATE THINKING is one of the important foundation stones of all enduring success. This lesson teaches you how to separate "facts" from mere "information." It teaches you how to organize known facts into two classes: the "important" and the "unimportant." It teaches you how to determine what is an "important" fact. It teaches you how to build definite working plans, in the pursuit of any calling, out of FACTS.

XI.     CONCENTRATION teaches you how to focus your attention upon one subject at a time until you have worked out practical plans for mastering that subject. It will teach you how to ally yourself with others in such a manner that you may have the use of their entire knowledge to back you up in your own plans and purposes. It will give you a practical working knowledge of the forces around you, and show you how to harness and use these.

XII.     CO-OPERATION will teach you the value of team-work in all you do. In this lesson you will be taught how to apply the law of the "Master Mind" described in this Introduction and in Lesson Two of this course. This lesson will show you how to co-ordinate your own efforts with those of others, in such a manner that friction, jealousy, strife, envy and cupidity will be eliminated. You will learn how to make use of all that other people have learned about the work in which you are engaged.

XIII.     PROFITING BY FAILURE will teach you how to make stepping stones out of all of your past and future mistakes and failures. It will teach you the difference between "failure" and "temporary defeat," a difference which is very great and very important. It will teach you how to profit by your own failures and by the failures of other people.

XIV.     TOLERANCE will teach you how to avoid the disastrous effects of racial and religious prejudices which mean defeat for millions of people who permit themselves to become entangled in foolish argument over these subjects, thereby poisoning their own minds and closing the door to reason and investigation. This lesson is the twin sister of the one on ACCURATE THOUGHT, for the reason that no one may become an Accurate Thinker without practicing tolerance. Intolerance closes the book of Knowledge and writes on the cover, "Finis! I have learned it all!" Intolerance makes enemies of those who should be friends. It destroys opportunity and fills the mind with doubt, mistrust and prejudice.

XV.     PRACTICING THE GOLDEN RULE will teach you how to make use of this great universal law of human conduct in such a manner that you may easily get harmonious co-operation from any individual or group of individuals. Lack of understanding of the law upon which the Golden Rule philosophy is based is one of the major causes of failure of millions of people who remain in misery, poverty and want all their lives. This lesson has nothing whatsoever to do with religion in any form, nor with sectarianism, nor have any of the other lessons of this course on the Law of Success.

When you have mastered these Fifteen Laws and made them your own, as you may do within a period of from fifteen to thirty weeks, you will be ready to develop sufficient personal power to insure the attainment of your Definite Chief Aim.

# CHAPTER 6

## APPLYING POSITIVE THINKING TO THE 15 PRINCIPLES (LAW OF SUCCESS)

This section will deal with the relationship between Napoleon Hill's 15 principles and the application of Positive Thinking.

1. ### *DEFINITE CHIEF AIM*

This represents the first principle of the Law of Success. It is universally believed that a chief aim is a prerequisite for achievement of success in any form. A chief aim or goal is like the rudder of a boat. Without a rudder, you can apply as much power as you wish but the boat cannot move. It will spin in the same place. Positive thinking translates this chief aim into a living, breathing reality. Once you have marked your territory and goal, you can use Positive thinking as a tool to keep you on track and to maintain 100 percent involvement with your goal. Positive thinking then reassures you that you have the power and enthusiasm to stay on track till your goal is accomplished.

2. ### *CULTIVATION OF SELF-CONFIDENCE*

Principle 2 is the cultivation of Self-Confidence, which results by mastering the six basic fears. Napoleon Hill expressed these six very real fears as: "the six basic fears with which every person is cursed------the fear of Poverty, the fear of Ill-Health, the fear of Old Age, the fear of Criticism, the fear of Loss of Love of Someone and the fear of Death." What role does Positive Thinking play in the elimination of these six fears? Let us look at one of these fears in more detail: the fear of Poverty. The Fear of Poverty is a real fear for a lot of people. There are some who have been born and raised in a poor family and have experienced many difficulties in merely surviving economically. There are others at the extreme opposite of the economic spectrum, who are very wealthy, but still fear that one day they will lose it all. Positive thinking for the poor is the promise that they can change their future. Along with positive thinking, they need to believe they are truly worthy of change and choose to ignore the rumblings of all negative people around them.

It is true that the poor have less choices in terms of immediately changing their living, economic or social environment (than the wealthy). However, if there is a positive thought in their Life by them consciously believing that they deserve more and will receive more, then Positive thinking will play a great role in helping pave their way for a better future. If, on the other hand, they think and act like most poor people, who project an attitude of lack and insufficiency accompanied with anger, hatred, despondency and depression, then such people will never be able to break out of the chains of poverty. The choice is essentially theirs: continue to live in pain and lack or work positively and think, act and feel positive to create a better Life for themselves. For the rich, the fear of becoming poor may sometimes project itself as an imaginary future Reality. These wealthy people have attached their self-worth, social standing and their power over others to the possession of wealth and the real fear here is what would happen to their false belief of self-security if their wealth suddenly collapses. Positive thinking for such people will only work if they shift their attitude and consciousness to a feeling of self-worth based on what they are and what they believe in and shift their attachment away from money to that of self- worth based on their values and their contributions to others.

3.    ***HABIT OF SAVING***

Principle 3 proposes the inculcation at an early age of the habit of saving. Saving money has become difficult, if not impossible in this day and age. As the cost of all goods and services increase dramatically(while income stagnates), there is a real challenge to save anything. In North America, the vast proportion of the population pay their bills on a month-to-month cycle. Very few North Americans have more than a few thousand dollars in their savings account —--most of the populace rely on their credit card to fund short-term financial emergencies. In such a dire situation, how does one save? There are two and only two ways to save money: ***one is to earn more and the second is to spend less***.

For most working class people, a sudden increase in income is not possible, so the only practical means to save is by spending less. And this involves making the sacrifice of doing without things they may be used to, in exchange for creation of a savings and wealth portfolio, which will generate some sense of future financial security. The role of positive thinking in money savings and accumulation is to provide the person with the strength and courage to start that savings journey now.

If positive thinking is projected with a sense of future economic security and well-being then there is a real possibility that one can save some money for a better financial future. If you can picture an adequate amount of future wealth to help you fortify against unknown emergencies like job loss, poor health resulting in high medical bills and also the promise of money to fund down payment of a new home or funding for college education of a child, in addition to enough to live comfortably when you retire, then positive thinking can play a role in creating and maintaining the savings habit.

## 4.   _INITIATIVE AND LEADERSHIP_

Principle 4 talks about the creation of initiative and leadership as you enlist others to your cause------ leading to fulfillment of your personal success. Positive thinking in terms of creating and expressing novel and unique ideas to improve a situation at say, your work place, will result in more people noticing you and your contribution. And how do you actually go about employing Positive thinking in this purpose? It is by always staying positive at work, by encouraging your co-employees to stay positive and look at the bright side of things, to creating your personal view that any obstacles are surmountable at work (by suggesting positive and efficient ways of solving problems). The more positive you think, act and feel in relationship with your co-workers, bosses and the changing situation at work, the greater the aura of leadership you create, which helps you maintain initiative and control over your destiny. As I have always said, the real challenge you face is within yourself: if you understand that being positive will make you stand out from the crowd, if you believe that positive thinking will assist you in becoming more indispensable to your company and if you see that continual use of positive thinking will create a natural leadership position in your work environment, then you will work more hard at staying positive all the time.

## 5.   _IMAGINATION_

Principle 5 deals with the use of imagination in creating a success field for yourself. Can you use positive thinking to fuel imagination? Definitely, you can.

So, first, if you can picture in advance that you have a positive imagination field, then you give yourself the permission to think outside the box. Once you come up with new and unique ways of working and relating to others, then you continue to use positive thinking in such new directions. This is a unique adaptation of the power of positive thinking.

6.    *ENTHUSIASM*

Principle 6 deals with generating enthusiasm in everything you do. How is positive thinking playing a role here? You can adopt the use of Positive thinking in two roles, one of which is constructive and the other destructive:

The destructive expression of positive thinking is the mere adoption of a passive, non-excited way of expressing positivism. This is done by some individuals who feel that mere positive thinking will get them places without the additional use of effort and knowledge.

The second more constructive approach is to use effort, knowledge and visualization, combining all these vital factors in a positive fashion. The second approach calls for you to really be excited and enthusiastic about being positive. You just feel happy that you have lofty goals and you are enthused to working to achieve them. Your enthusiasm will catch like wildfire in whatever environment you are in. So positive thinking accompanied with enthusiasm with strong visualization accompanied with a belief you deserve what you strive for will create the magic formula for your success.

7.    *SELF-CONTROL*

Principle 7 expresses the fact that self-control is essential to long-term success. If you understand that the road to Success is a journey and not necessarily one end destination, that you in your lifetime will have multiple goals worthy of achievement, you will understand how important it is to plan your time and maintain self-control over your energy. An awareness of the importance of self-control, while exercising constant positive thinking will assist you in discovering success. So, when you get distracted and get caught doing something which is not that important to your success, then you need to bring back positive thinking and maintain this thinking in the constant direction of your pre-determined goal, not straying away from your long-term focus.

8. ***HABIT OF DOING MORE THAN YOU ARE PAID FOR***

Principle 8 deals with the effect of doing more than you are paid for. This principle coincides with the Law of Action and Reaction. This Newtonian Law basically says that every action has an equal and opposite reaction, a Law which has been scientifically proven. In the non-physical world of Action, all effort invested by an individual is bound to create an equivalent amount of result. However, the twist in this principle is that you do more than you are asked or paid for to do, knowing that by doing more upfront, you are contributing more to someone else's betterment.

It also means that you know that sooner or later you will be rewarded for that extra effort. But the important thing here is that you do not do more now, hoping to gain a greater benefit in the future. You just do more because it is the right thing to do. This is the philosophical aspect of this principle and it always works. Positive thinking can be now viewed as a process for not only an individual's fulfillment, but also a process to help other. So if you can use positive thinking for the benefit of others in greater proportion than what you seek to expect from such thought, you will work in consistency with this principle.

9. ***PLEASING PERSONALITY***

Principle 9 calls for maintaining a pleasing personality in all contact with other people and situations. Positive thinking should allow you to visualize a happy personal situation, and when you feel at ease with yourself and your Life, then you instantly project this ease towards others. This creates a pleasing personality---- one which allows others to work with you cooperatively.

10. ***ACCURATE THINKING***

Principle 10 deals with the role of Accurate thinking in assuring personal Success. Accurate thinking is the ability to distinguish facts from fiction. Before you start applying the power of positive thinking, you must be sure that you are engaging in the promotion of factual information. If you apply positive thinking to fiction or delusional thought, you will get results attached to such predominant thought.

Positive thinking in the direction of factual information will result in success, while positive thinking in an imagined fictional direction has the ability to lead you nowhere. So selectivity in application of positive thinking is critical in terms of getting what you want.

## 11. _CONCENTRATION_

Principle 11 deals with the importance of concentration in achieving Success. Concentration is the ability to focus all your energy towards your chosen task necessary for you to reach your goal. Constancy in positive thinking in the direction of your chosen task is vital for success creation.

## 12. _COOPERATION_

Principle 12 explains the value of enlisting cooperation and its role in your personal Success. Cooperation deals with signing up others to all activities, which lead to your future Success. And this understanding involves the acceptance of a symbiotic relationship between you and your other significant work or personal partners. It also means that you realize that you do not use co-operation as a devious way to artificially excite others to your cause, only dropping them when you have reached your goal.

It is the enlightened understanding that your Success is linked to someone else's and that your attitude towards cooperation results in a win-win situation for everyone. You can now influence your chosen environment by committing yourself to 100% positivism in every act involving cooperation with others. If others get excited by your cause and truly believe this will lead to their personal growth then you will have no problem in using positive thinking to harvesting cooperation in your endeavors.

## 13.    _PROFITING FROM FAILURE_

Principle 13 discusses how one can profit from failure and use this experience as a building block for future Success. This approach challenges you to only make a mistake once(in a specific, given situation). I have always believed that you are entitled to one mistake in a certain field of action. The challenge is that you need to learn from that mistake and therefore set up conditions which prevents a repetition of a similar mistake in the future. Positive thinking can assist in this regard. The understanding here must be clear that positive thinking is a tool which must be used wisely in your Life.

If things do not go your way, it is not the fault of positive thinking, but merely a sign of how you have approached a particular challenge in your Life. It could be faulty execution, an unrealistic goal, lack of cooperation from others, etcetera. You need to continue employing positive thinking but explore the real reasons behind a short-term failing. And remember a failing is not a permanent failure till you choose to regard it that way. Use positive thinking to shed light on the true causes of short-term failing and continue applying positive thinking even after discovery of the failing. What I am trying to say here is that positive thinking is a given and standard form of mental and emotional communication, which must be used in good times and bad.

14. **_TOLERANCE_**

Principle 14 calls for exercising tolerance in all relationships. Positive thinking, when combined with the power of forgiveness and empathy help create this sense and attitude of tolerance towards others. To understand no one is perfect and that certain individuals or situations may conspire against your goals short-term, is the most healthy attitude and approach. A belief in your abilities and goals, an implicit faith in the power of positive thinking and an understanding of the miraculous impact of tolerance will assist in always creating long-term success, even when the road may appear bleak and blurry in the short run.

15. **_THE GOLDEN RULE_**

Principle 15 talks about the Golden Rule. This is a biblical rule, which says the following: "Do unto others the way you expect to be done unto you." If you employ positive thinking with this attitude, if you truly believe that in addition to the exercise of positive thought that you are simultaneously sending you good and kind feelings towards others, which you know will be reciprocated, then you set up the necessary conditions for more cooperation and success in your Life.

# CHAPTER 7

## UNDERSTANDING THE LAW OF SUB-CONSCIOUS POWER

### (also known as The Power of the Sub-Conscious Mind)

The Law of Sub-Conscious Power is best explained by Dr. Joseph Murphy in his landmark book, "The Power of your Mind." In this unbelievable and awesome book, Dr. Murphy very clearly expresses the fact that there are two levels to the Mind: the conscious objective Mind, which is involved in our day to day Living decisions and a hidden Sub-Conscious Mind which is the subjective aspect of Life (and is also the seat of Divinity).

Here is my take on the vital discovery and understanding of the Mind: We have two aspects to our Life, one known and one unknown. It is most unfortunate that we live our Life in one compartment predominantly-----the compartment most familiar to us and which is normally in use and under our control: the conscious Mind. However, unknown to us is a *vast "mental/emotional" apparatus* buried deep in our mental ocean: a sub-conscious power, which controls most of our Actions. We ignorantly believe we are in control of everything around us through the exercise of the conscious faculty----- this Conscious Mind, though is mysteriously and totally controlled by the submerged entity, known as the sub-conscious Mind. What makes it difficult for us to fathom this sub-conscious is the lack of a body of knowledge to tap into it with a view to understanding its structure----as a result, our understanding of the power of the sub-conscious is merely superficial. Where we seem to come in touch with it is through sudden expression of feelings of happiness or sadness and depression, which indicate how we are doing in our Life at a particular moment in time. These feelings then control how we act on the conscious level. Even though we do not understand the sub-conscious, we must try as much as we can, to fathom its content. This, for many, is a Lifelong challenge and a difficult one at best.

If you accept the premise of the Power of the Sub-Conscious Mind, then you are one step closer to work with this Power. This is really a complementary power you possess and not something to be afraid of ----- nor is it a Power, which gets understood by theorization. This Power needs to be felt through constant Awareness and Understanding. The presence of feeling being generated through the Sub-Conscious Power is not only proof of its existence but also of its intangible dominion over your Life----- it is your immediate and direct contact with this mysterious subconscious.

If, at some point in your Life, you feel lousy or unhappy and you realize something is wrong in your Life, then you see the mirror of the sub-conscious as it reflect itself on your conscious Mind. So the question which arises now is, "How is one to harness the power of the sub-conscious to defeat your sadness? How can you make your sub-conscious mind your friend and ally and not your opponent? Is there a way to understand this mysterious ocean of Power? And after understanding this power, is there a possibility of harnessing its energy for your beneficial use? The answers to all these questions is ——-" Yes, it is really possible." There is a great opportunity and possibility to access this hidden Power, but only if you have an open, non-judgmental Mind and approach.

The mechanism for communication with the sub-conscious is through he conscious. To reach the deeper layers of the mind (in order to tap this power), you need to start with the conscious mind, since this is the only place we can start from. The next chapter will indicate all the wonderful and powerful techniques you can use to tap this power---- and make this Power work in your Life. And all this will be done in relationship to your understanding of the power of Positive thinking, which works in tandem with this powerful Law of Sub-Conscious Power.

# CHAPTER 8

## THE SUB-CONSCIOUS POWER-

### "A MIRACLE OF POSITIVE THINKING"

This chapter deals with an understanding of how to tap your sub-conscious power and in this process invites positive thinking to our conversation. The     sub-conscious power can only be tapped indirectly. This is a very important fact to understand. The relationship between the conscious and sub-conscious is intricate and hidden. Thought vibrations emanating from the conscious centers of the brain, get stored in the sub-conscious memory center. This memory center lodges all experiences of joy and pain, hurt and anger, jealously and depression. When situations appear on our horizon, which match similar experiences in the past, then identical reactions and feelings get evoked. This therefore makes us incapable of seeing a new situation in our Life with child like freshness; we are always interpreting what is happening to us with respect to our past framework of experience, which is stored indelibly in our hidden brain center. So, Life becomes a repetition of one similar experience superimposed on a past similar experience. This unfortunately becomes our constant Reality moving from an experience from our past into the present and reflecting itself into the future.

If one wants to make a fresh start in Life, you need to forget about the past and its impressions on your cerebral center. This is easily said than done, since thought is always interfering with our perception of Reality---- what I mean by this is that we see Life through our own special rose colored lens. This rose colored lens is our interpretation of Life and not Reality. However, we experience it as Reality and accept it as such. If there is a possibility of a massive change in External life result, then one needs to find a new way of experiencing whatever is happening in the form of Life results on the outside periphery of our Existence.

So let us start this journey by giving you a real Life example. You want to own a house and create your own happiness and security there with your family. However, unknown to you, you have been doing things, thinking thoughts which work in creating a lack of positive result of home ownership. You have not been able to attract the kind of house and home you desire. How do you now attract what you desire? First by acknowledging the fact that you are doing something wrong now. And then opening up to the possibility of making mental and emotional changes to make your dream come true.

The mechanism to get what you want is through a process I label as "mental impregnation". By this, I mean a process where you bombard your conscious mind with suggestions that you already have what you desire. So, if your dream is to own a home, you go to a builder's office in the area where you desire this home and get floor plans/pictures of the house you wish to live in. Pin this picture in numerous places in your existing house, your car, your office and all the places where you would look at it often. The more you experience and believe that you already own and live in this home, the faster it will enter your Reality.

In addition, you need to create positive affirmations to assist you in the dream attraction process. What is an affirmation? It is a prayer embedded in faith where you invoke the blessings of the Universe to get you what you want in the shortest possible time, without inflicting pain on others. If you can visualize your Energy powerhouse as residing in your very own sub-conscious, if you can understand and implement this process of activating the sub-conscious in alignment with your dream, if you can affirm your belief which is now rooted in prayer and the utmost faith, you open up yourself to the possibility of receiving what you want from the outside.

One very important principle, which needs to be understood is that all material things in the universe can be attracted by you, "the dreamer". And the attraction process starts in your Mind. If you positively accept that you deserve what you want and that by invoking blessings by superimposing positive expectant thoughts/feelings (on your conscious mind) by constant repetition will allow these suggestions to pass on to your sub-conscious------the power of such subconscious suggestion will work in the external world to attract toward you all the objects of your affection. So, if you feel unhappy, you affirm you are happy now. If you are poor, you affirm you are wealthy now and thank the Universe for your Life and wealth. This now sets up a counteracting energy force and the Power of the Sub-conscious mind goes into work and makes you start the journey from poverty to wealth by attracting situations, people and experiences on the outside(your Life) to help you get what you want.

What is the miracle of Positive thinking to do with the Power of the Sub-conscious? Positive thinking, in this context, becomes a tool to help you get where you want to go in the shortest possible time with the least amount of obstacle and pain. Positive thinking, positive affirmations and positive visualization are utilized on a regular basis to impress your sub-conscious with all the things you desire and then the power of the sub-conscious goes to work for you, rather automatically, to help you get what you truly wish. In a contrary vein, one has to be very careful not to invoke the opposite of positive thinking, which is negative thought. For example, if you dream and focus on your poverty then using these methods and techniques will not work. The mind gets what it wishes for and the more negative you think of a particular subject the more the sub-conscious draws the same negativism and lack of result into your Life.

Therefore a constant and ever-expanding positive awareness with positive affirmations, visualization and prayer will help you reach the point in Life where you feel most happy and fulfilled. You must allow this new Discovery into your Life---- so not only have you to visualize your new Future, but you need to have the utmost faith in such change in your Life. And, in addition, you must intend this result to touch your Life. Positive prayer and affirmation, Positive intent and utmost faith accompanied with positive suggestion will allow the Sub-Conscious power to work a miracle in your Life.

# CHAPTER 9

## UNDERSTANDING THE LAW OF PSYCHO-CYBERNETICS

In his brilliant book, entitled, 'Psycho-Cybernetics," Dr, Maxwell Maltz propounded a very important theory. But before we discuss this theory, let us talk a little about the pioneering plastic surgeon, Dr. Maxwell Maltz. This renowned surgeon was world famous and specialized in making people look and feel beautiful. By his miraculous medical and surgical talent, Dr. Maltz specialized (through surgery) to make remarkable changes in people's physical beings. But with time, Dr. Maltz started to question the value of his contribution to his patients. Was sculpting faces and bodies, the be all and end all of Life? Was there a better way to assist his patients live a more fuller and complete Life? After great contemplation, Dr. Maltz embarked on a new medical adventure with his prospective clients. Before he initiated a surgical procedure, he committed to an initial psychological exploratory session with his potential client. In this session, he went deep into the question of why this patient wanted a smaller or bigger nose or a different shaped breast. Dr. Maltz now went into the subject of self- concept v self-image. This was to fully educate the patient beforehand of the advantages and disadvantages of surgical procedure in terms of fulfillment of what they wanted. We will now discuss this theory in the next paragraph.

Central to Dr. Maltz's theory was an investigation into the underlying reason behind a patient's need to look better physically. In many instances, he saw this as a superficial way of looking better from his patient's point of view. For example, he would ask a prospective patient what the process of breast enhancement represented in real terms to her. Would they feel beautiful with this plastic surgery? What else could they do to look and feel beautiful? A lot of his new pioneering work had to do with examining the feelings and self-worth of his patients with a view to enabling them to understand that, for example, real beauty is not skin deep. By examining their real needs, expectations, fears and anxieties about their bodies, Dr. Maltz contributed by enlightening his patients to seeing what and why they were so preoccupied by their bodies. In the process he created a better sense of direction and motivation for his clients.

He no longer became a doctor in business to make money by meeting the perceived needs of his clients, but became a true doctor who examined the feelings, motivations and desires of his clients and assisted them in understanding themselves better so that if they still decided to undertake facial or body surgery that they understood the value and significance of this process. And he also helped them enlarge their vision as how the proposed surgery fit in with their bigger vision of Life.

Dr. Maltz's work led to deep and intensive psychological work which differentiated the understanding and borders between self-concept and self-image. Very simply, self-concept is how you see yourself as being and self-image is how you see the world seeing you. In numerous instances, Dr. Maltz's patients were revealed a story on their private and exclusive self-concept and self-image. A self-concept of a lady who wanted to have breast enhancement was that she looked awful with small breasts versus her self image which saw her view her friends as seeing her as ugly and unattractive due to her small breasts and that by enlarging her breasts she would win their approval. Do note that in this story, the woman first was touched by her self-image, which is her view of ugliness as directly related to the size of her breasts, which prompted her to create and support her self-concept. If, through analysis, she understood on her own that her understanding of beauty was not merely restricted to the size of her breasts, then the self-concept would go through a dramatic change. Her understanding of her true beauty would not allow this concept to take hold and strengthen inside herself and would negate the very poor self-concept she held now as a direct relationship of her association of her breast size with her concept of her personal beauty. If the understanding was complete, then there may not have been a need for breast enlargement surgery.

The challenge here was to focus on the self-concept of the patient first and to make the patient live their life with emphasis on their self-concept as opposed to her self-image (or how they felt the world viewed them). In the process, Dr. Maltz enlarged the vision of his patients and truly touched their emotional, mental and physical motivations prompting their perceived need for surgery.

# CHAPTER 10

## APPLYING PRINCIPLES OF POSITIVE THINKING TO PSYCHO-CYBERNETICS

The great contribution of Dr. Maltz was in his urging his patients to have a much closer look at themselves, mentally, physically and emotionally. More emphasis was placed on their true needs as determined by them solely and an avoidance of having their Life and resultant actions controlled by their image of what others may think best for them.

This type of thinking really leads up to and is intrinsically related to the Law of Attraction, the Law of Success and the Law of the Sub-Conscious Mind. The challenge faced by humans is determining what they truly want and deserve 4 universal laws challenged humans to independently craft a Life strategy to get what they want, easily and effortlessly. In this process of goal formulation and plan of action, great conflict is faced by most practitioners particularly when family, friends and society do not view such endeavor and goal setting favorably.

Positive thinking assists a success seeker stay on course and believe in his self-formulated dreams, desires and goals. It provides him the courage to stay on course and withstand all rejections and conflict from his immediate environment. Positive thinking, through reinforcement also assists the practitioner from daring to dream his own dream and taking the steps required to be successful in his own right and time. And most importantly, association of positive thinking with a constant and complete awareness of these 4 laws assures complete and unconditional success in all endeavors.

And the ultimate and eventual dream of positive thinking is to create such a strong image of a person's purpose and Life vision, that through his actions he makes the world see him the way he sees and feels himself. In this respect his self-concept wins over his self-image. This is the highest level of self-visualization and corresponds to a totally self-actualized state in the Maslowian need pyramid(associated with celebrated psychologist, Dr. Maslow). Here is a person who knows what he wants, who has the courage to walk his own path amidst resistance from without and crafts his own special place in the Sun where he achieves all his expressed needs with a sense of ease in complete harmony and Peace with his surrounding. He now controls his environment and never does his environment dominate him.

-PAGE LEFT BLANK INTENTIONALLY-

THIS PAGE LEFT INTENTIONALLY EMPTY

# SECTION 2

## -THE BASICS

THIS PAGE LEFT BLANK INTENTIONALLY

48

# CHAPTER 11

## WHY YOU SHOULD THINK AND ACT POSITIVELY

Life is a wonderful yet mysterious journey. On your journey you discover many friends and enemies; you encounter happiness and tragedy---- you go through so many ups and downs. Sometimes you wonder what this trip is all about. Nothing makes sense but the way you approach and receive all these myriads of experiences. In fact, Life is nothing but a series of relationships, some meaningful, some hopeful, and others distant and disconnected with your Life. As you strive to superimpose your wishes and dreams on the naked external world, you have some success and many failures. You strive to improve your batting ratio; you want to experience and enjoy Life with more happy and balanced Relationships. In this context, Positive thinking is the gateway to a meaningful future.

Let me explain why. Man is faced with both good and evil. And there is always a choice. And this choice has to do with not only how he reacts to his External Life results but how he chooses to live every moment of his Life. Ultimately, you can choose to be in one of three states: Positive, Accepting or Negative. Let us talk about these three essential choices: Positive indicates a happy, passionate approach to Life, where you hope and execute the very best plans for your future in a spirit of harmony and cooperation. Accepting is the middle ground, where you just let Life just take you where it pushes you. The winds of Time and Space push you in so many directions, some good, some bad and some just of no real significance. The third choice is a negative choice where you choose to look at the negative side of things happening to you now and project these negative feelings into the future through anxiety, anger, hatred and depression. When you look at your Life and survey the three choices you have, it is easy to ascertain that the best choice for optimal Life result is to be positive and stay positive all the time ------ this will attract what you seek faster and create a Life blessed with purpose, harmony and happiness.

On the other hand if you are passive, you submit to the forces of Karma and then get caught up in a whirlwind of action and reaction with results coming in directions you may or may be happy with. Or if you choose to stay negative, then future results expand in a negative direction. Hatred, anger, anxiety and depression create matching results in the future through the intervention of the sub-conscious mind. The sub-conscious mind picks up these vibrations, which get stored in its memory drive and then manifest results corresponding to these negative emotions, values and attitudes.

Given all the stress and strain of Life accompanied with the massive personal, economic and financial uncertainty facing us, you must take up the challenge of creating your own future and happiness. And what better way to do it than through the miracle of Positive Thought, Affirmation and Prayer?????

# CHAPTER 12

## DECIDE WHAT YOU WANT

The first step in your journey towards a happy and successful Life is your determination of what you truly want to be complete and fulfilled. And there is no hard and fast way of determining this. Every person is specially crafted and therefore must craft his own special unique, innate direction. In terms of selecting a choice destination, one must look at all aspects of his Life----- his career, his family, his Love life, his hobbies, his passions and his very special inclinations. What would make you feel totally fulfilled in this Miracle called Life? If you had a magic wand and could create anything you wished out of thin air, what would you choose to have? What would you choose to do and be? How would you like to feel, right now as a result of fulfillment of your dreams, desires and wishes?

This will now bring us to the subject of goal setting. This is the crux of the decision making process. The first stage is to write down what you truly want. You may start by taking a plain piece of foolscap paper and write down quite randomly what you really want in terms of concrete goals. If you cannot do that easily, then just write down on paper your mental picture of what kind of life you    choose. Remember, if you do not choose what you want from your Life, someone else will make that decision for you, whether it be your parents, your immediate family, your society and/or your Government. This choice is not to be left to anyone but yourself. In free open democratic societies, individuals have a lot more choices than in authoritarian or communist regimes. So if you are born and living in a free democratic country that is a great starting point.

Once you list all your goals, then prioritize them with 1 being the most important and the last number on your list as the least important. Another way of doing this exercise is first setting up separate Life chapters and then underlining your goals under each chapter. So you can divide your Life chapters into: Personal, family, career/avocation, hobbies, passions, financial, charitable pursuits, etcetera and then under each category write your Life goals.

These goals once surveyed and finalized represent your first Life path. This is why you are doing what you are doing and this represents your meaning, purpose and fulfillment in Life. This goal book must always be referred to evaluate your progress towards accomplishing what you set out to. Without goals, life is meaningless and without purpose-----goal formulation and prioritization is the first and best point in terms of starting your journey towards getting what you want.

# CHAPTER 13

## BELIEVE YOUR GOAL IS ACHIEVABLE

After you have formulated and prioritized your goals, then you work towards achievement of such goals. The important question here is: "Do you believe your goals are achievable? Are you setting goals which you do not believe in? Or do you feel you do not set goals because these will probably never happen?" One rule I learnt early on in my Life, was to first set small goals rather than massive long-term goals. Try to first set up short-term goals and make these simple, so you can achieve them. Achievement of these goals will boost your self-confidence and move you towards establishing more loftier and exciting long-term goals.

If something is preventing you from sitting down and formulating your Life goals or if this process is marked with uncertainty, fear and lack of belief, you need to delve further into your psyche. What is stopping you from being what you want to be? What is stopping you from even starting your journey by writing down these goals? Has there been any negative Life experience with which you are associating which prevents you from starting your journey towards success? You must and you can meet this challenge by stroking the sub-conscious with positive thoughts and prayer and affirmation at the conscious mind level thus opening up your sub conscious power to manifest your goals.

Remember Rome was not built in a day and your constant work, positivism and perseverance will help you assemble the pieces of the puzzle called your Life in a way where things happen just the way you want it to. Just believe in the process and have immense faith and you will move mountains.

# CHAPTER 14

## BELIEVE IN YOURSELF

Everything starts and ends with self-belief. I am talking about the kind of self-belief, which moves mountains, which gives you the courage to move forward in the face of resistance. Finding, holding on and developing this courage and self-belief is most important in your life journey.

First you must believe you have this courage---- and if not, you must believe that you can garner your sub-conscious power to reach this energy station. It is known for centuries untold that the more energy and passion you apply to your Life work the better the Life result. And when you combine this power with positive thinking, results flow quickly. Now what if you do not feel you have this power nor do you possess the complete and unconditional feeling of total self-belief. This is an area where you must get to work immediately. It will be interesting to note what kind of feelings and thoughts come to the surface when you ask yourself if you totally believe yourself. If the feeling of insufficiency is strong, then meditation is a good recipe. Very simply, to start the meditative process, sit quietly in a room where there is no distraction of any kind whatsoever. No television, no internet and no cell phone. Just you and your inner presence. And then watch what kind of thoughts and feeling come to the surface. If through this meditative process, you can try to see if there are reasons why you feel the way you do based on your past experience, result, family background etcetera, that would be an important first step in your self-discovery process. Once you isolate these factors, you need to positively negate them. That is, you accept they are in your Life now but you will release it from your consciousness and give the negative pattern away. Once you release it, then you superimpose your positive expectations of Life in the presence of your written Life goals.

Work at positive prayer and affirmation, superimposing your new values to align with your new goals and new self-confidence. Remember you will not get to where you want to go quickly if you carry your old baggage with you. Self limiting thoughts and beliefs, false conditioning's and fear work in direct opposition to positive thought and affirmation. So instead of choosing to focus on your self insufficiency, try to set them aside, even if you can achieve this on a temporary basis------ now you shift focus to your new written Life goals, including your new affirmations and re-visit your total faith in what you want; allow the newness to enter your Life and by positive stroking of the conscious allow the power of the sub-conscious Mind to work miracles in your Life through its partnership with Positive thought.

# CHAPTER 15

## HAVE A POSITIVE MENTAL ATTITUDE

Napoleon Hill in his book, "Think and Grow Rich," constantly refers to the process of building a positive mental attitude and how this helps you achieve success in any field you choose. This is a must read for all aspiring success seekers. A Positive Mental Attitude is a prerequisite for success in any field. The more positive you are, the easier it is for you to attract what you wish. Now we have heard this saying so many times----- but have we really employed it to transform our Life? Not really. The challenge is not only reading about what Napoleon Hill and numerous New Age thought leaders mention. The real challenge is to transform the meaning of this saying in your Life so that application of a Positive Mental Attitude is accompanied with much success in your Life. And how is one to do this? By constant and eternal self vigilance?

Positive thinking is very difficult to maintain at all points of time. A person may be judged by how many hours a day he engages in positive thought. Because if he slips his guard the devils of anxiety, stress, anger and hatred present themselves along with their sisters of self-doubt and fear. To be in a 100 % positive mental mode, one needs to challenge oneself constantly. But one cannot challenge oneself in a vacuum. Read the autobiographies of some of the great leaders of our times; the stories of Mahatma Gandhi, Martin Luther King and John F. Kennedy. All these powerful and successful people never gave up on their dream of freedom, fairness, equality and justice in spite of all the negative pressures around them. They are models pointing us towards their ever present light---- their fulfillment of a Life of meaning and significance should stir us to greater heights even if we can only learn from their Life history.

And without Positive Mental attitude, all is lost. As hard as you may try, the results will not be in your favor or if they are, it will take much time, trial and tribulation. Why not start today to build a positive mental attitude. Promise yourself you will be the best you can be. Arm yourself with a high dose of energy and self-confidence. And see in your inner eye, the fulfillment of your Life vision before it even happens. Allow that new experience in. And dare to be different. Positive mental attitude is the elixir of Life---- the magic wand which can move you quickly in the direction of your dream and desire.

# CHAPTER 16

## BE AN INVERSE PARANOID

A Paranoid is typically understood as someone who projects a negative experience into his presence. This happens due to the projection of negative and undesirable thought and feeling about any Life situation. An inverse paranoid is someone who, through conscious action, does the opposite of what a paranoid would do in any given challenging situation. So if a paranoid would run away from a difficult situation in Life, an inverse paranoid would do the exact opposite in terms of action. He would go head on and face the headwinds with courage and enthusiasm, knowing he will prevail.

Therefore, with the assistance of positive thinking, these are few of the concrete and energetic action moves an inverse paranoid can engage in:

1.      Taking constant and consistent action to achieve his written goals.

2.      Accepting fear and uncertainty in the environment but taking action anyway.

3.      Be willing to pay the price in advance for fulfillment of his Life dream.

4.      Gathering the strength and courage to reject rejection by focusing on his goal and not on what others may say about him or his actions, thoughts or feelings.

5.      Make a commitment to constant and never ending improvement.

6       Keeping constant score of success in his efforts to accomplish his goals.

7       Constant practice of persistence.


An inverse paranoid challenges his Life environment and acts in a positive manner every moment and second of his life---- he projects the reality of his intended future through all action taken by him. By negating fear and procrastination and by constant and vigorous application of all his action steps he succeeds in creating a winning situation for himself. And Positive Thinking is the strongest tool under his command to help him get to where he wants to go in the shortest time possible.

# CHAPTER 17

## TAKE ACTION AND KEEP SCORE

Now you have done all the hard yet passionate work. You have set your goals in writing. You have committed to them. You have set a specific time deadline to achieve all of them. You have established individual plans of action for each goal, marking the steps you must take to achieve them. You have employed a positive mental attitude as you move along your Life journey. And you have allowed and intended the desired changes to manifest themselves in your Life.

Now you need to take action and keep score of how quickly and efficiently you are arriving at your destination. This monitoring process must happen at least once a week. Do not be discouraged if it takes you some time to perfect your goal setting and achievement process. The critical part is you start and then you continue engaging in positive action never slowing down till your reach your final destination goal.

Along the way will come numerous obstacles, some setbacks and a few negative troughs accompanied with unkind emotions. You need to set aside all negative doubts, fears and misgiving and continue plodding to the end, with hope, passion and enthusiasm. And you dreams will come true, only because you believe in them and you allow your unconditional faith and prayer to get you where you need to be by harnessing the power of the sub-conscious and application of the positive thinking miracle.

THIS PAGE LEFT INTENTIONALLY BLANK

# SECTION 3

## -POSITIVE THINKING & RELATIONSHIPS

THIS PAGE LEFT INTENTIONALLY BLANK

# CHAPTER 18

## POSITIVISM AND INNER CONVICTION

Inner conviction is the magical power, which makes you totally believe in yourself. For most, it is a gift from Heaven. A few have this special quality gifted through their genetic, environmental and family conditioning. But there is no need to lose hope. Inner conviction is a quality which can be cultivated.

Inner conviction works alongside with hope. Where there is hope for change in the future, there are the implanted seeds for development of inner conviction. It is said that most change in human lives happen in times of adversity and great suffering. Now is the opportunity for you to seize this challenge and instead of hiding from pain and suffering and running away from Life's challenges, let us make a conversion of this situation to one where (with Hope) you create the fruits of Inner Conviction.

And what is Inner Conviction? It is a spirit of trust in the Universe and an ability to believe and hold steadfast in your Mind that you can and will attract what you desire. It is the spirit of allowing goodness accompanied with positive change in your Life. It is the strength to withstand and conquer great Life difficulties which may occur at any point in your life.

And how does Inner Conviction work with Positive Thinking? Positive thinking is the first step which launches he process of inner conviction. With positive thought you invite a new spirit within you---- this spirit of inner conviction then launches you into a new outlook towards all challenges in your Life. It then fuels a trust and self-belief, which gives you the power to not only withstand difficult Life conditions, but also provides a pathway to attraction of your most keenly felt and desired goals.

# POSITIVISM AND INSOMNIA

Insomnia is a condition, which affects people worldwide. It is basically a negative feeling, which is accompanied with restlessness-----this prevents you from sleeping well at night. I have talked to numerous people and there is this common strand of truth behind this condition---- people cannot go to sleep at an appointed time; while sleeping they cannot rest and relax but lie in their conscious mind condition or some get some sleep and wake up in the middle of the night and then cannot fall back to sleep. Insomnia is a disease worldwide. Without adequate rest, the Mind cannot perform its functions optimally. So many insomniacs complain of feeling tired and listless. The challenge of overcoming Insomnia is related to Positive Thinking. Let us first talk a bit about the causes of Insomnia.

Insomnia is truly a psychosomatic condition, where the body and Mind stop functioning in unison. The Mind, which is either restless and angry due to negative activities/results occurring during the day or due to a hyper activism at work now refuses to respond to sleep. The other deeper psychological condition creating insomnia is the presence of anxiety and depression. The conscious Mind, in this condition, refuses to slow down and allow the Sub-Conscious Mind to take over in the passage called Sleep. The disturbances, thoughts and hyperactivity at the surface level of the Mind creates a major thought ripple,  which refuses to let up.

Most insomniacs react poorly to their inability to sleep well at night. They seem to try to force themselves to sleep, but this does not work well and thereby creating more resistance and tension. The appropriate first step to insomnia is to take a journey into your mind. Try to find out what is troubling you. This can be done most effectively through Meditation. When the Mind is quiet and relaxed and not associated with external activities like watching a movie, surfing the net, talking on a cell phone or being involved with something in your house, office or play place one has an opportunity to become aware of the source of disturbance. You now have a clear chance to see what is bothering you. In many cases, if you are able to identify the root cause of the disturbance, whether it be a poor relationship, a difficult business day or other relevant matter, the awareness itself assists in improving your sleep. This is because Awareness allows you to not only come in touch with the stressor, but also allows you to give yourself the power to release its negative effect on you. This is done by accepting the disturbance and allowing it for the time being to be where it is.

Then by application of positive thinking, positive visualization and imagery accompanied with trust in yourself and the Universe to solve the issue, you gather strength to face the disturbed conscious layer of the Mind. This awareness combined with meditation can solve this issue —----you now create a space within your energy framework------- this Space then assists in healing and overcoming the negative effects of Insomnia.

Positive thinking, positive affirmations, a trust in the Universe, a keen sense of non-stop awareness around your mental situation, particularly in watching your thoughts as the day rolls by will all assist in providing a framework to slow and calm the mind----- good sleep, a recharging of the Mind and an invigorated wake up will all assist in creating a more harmonious and happy day---- creating conditions which assist in you achieving all your daily objectives, while enjoying the wonderful moments in Life.

## POSITIVISM AND CONSTANCY

Constancy is the direct result of you remaining true to your Cause. And what is your Cause------ it is to maintain harmony, happiness and Love in all relationships. But this challenge is not easily attainable. Most people fail to realize that the level of their overall Life success is based on the consistency of energy application and this is where constancy comes in. Constancy means consistent, efficient application of energy directed towards a desired and pre-determined Life goal.

Most individuals do not cultivate the capacity to work consistently 100% of the time but seem to be distracted with all of Life's side distractions. In fact, the ability to work consistently is directly correlated with your inner motivation level, which in turn is influenced by the clarity of your reward system, the clarity of your predetermined Life goals, the level of passion and enthusiasm with which you do your work and the application of Positive thought. Desire plays a prominent role in the application of a constant stream of energy focus on your chosen activities and tasks. So you must ask yourself whether you have clarified the role of desire in reaching your assigned and written goals. Are you clear about what works for you desire wise in relationship to energy exertion? In other words, is your desire to reach a particular place in Life of adequate quality and intensity that it generates an adequate amount of inner motivation to get to where you want to go?

Without constancy in thought, feeling and resultant action, goal achievement becomes very hard. Imagine working for a few days or weeks towards your goal and then getting sidetracked in your effort. Now compare yourself to someone else who is working hard and dreaming and self-actualizing 100% of the time. Your result has no chance to match the unique self actualizer's results.

Therefore, to improve your constancy level, you need to understand what you have set out to do, why you are doing what you started working with and what your progress is so far with respect to goal achievement. You also need to analyze and be aware of how efficiently your activities are operating on a day to day basis. This is where Positive Thinking is helpful. With positive thinking, you can motivate yourself to stay on track. With Positive Thinking you can visualize that you are a self-actualizer(even though you may not be that now). Positive thinking becomes an inner motivator to assist you in changing tracks to help you become more successful faster.

# POSITIVISM AND OVERCOMING REJECTION

Rejection is one of the significant challenges one experiences on one's Road to Success. For as one moves ahead to gain what one wishes, there are invariably obstacles along the way. These road blocks prevent you from moving smoothly from point A to point B. These blocks come in the way of opposition to your actions from your near and dear ones, from conflicts at your workplace to unexpected challenges in your new business. How you overcome the psychological effects of rejection is critical to your long run Success.

Something I learned in Sales School, which stood me in good stead through the years was the inculcation of a new approach to Rejection. I was basically trained to understanding that when someone rejected my sales presentation or refused to grant me a sales appointment, that these qualified prospects were not rejecting me but the ideas I was putting forward. This became a revolutionary point for me psychologically as I strove to build a clientele. The reason I am sharing this story is because most people take someone telling them "No" as being a sign of personal rejection. They project that they may not be worthy of someone else in an intimate relationship or that they are not good in their job or business if they hear a lot of "No's". To me, as I matured into a professional salesperson, was the notion that the more "No's" I got the more "Yes's" would ensue. So, in a way, I invited the "No's" as a stepping stone to personal/professional success. Now all of you may not be comfortable with this idea; but please try it as it really works. When someone does not go along with you accept the "No," with grace and move on to fresher pastures.

What is the relationship between Positive Thinking and Rejection? Positive thinking assists in rejecting your Rejection by others. Let me explain how. If you are emotional and sensitive to how others react to you, particularly when they are in disagreement with your idea/ideas, you can use positive thinking to lessen the personal, psychological effects of such behavior. So, the next time someone rejects your idea and you feel bad, you supplant the negative thought/feeling by a positive thought/feeling. You need to be creative in this process. So, if your girlfriend walks away from your Life and you feel horrible, you now superimpose the thought/feeling that you have already found a better partner and you are deserving of a better relationship. This principle of superimposition always works if you give it a sincere try. You switch a negative feeling and supplant it with a positive thought/feeling.

In numerous situations in your Life, when things may not be going your way and you experience negative feelings, you merely supplant the negative feeling with a positive feeling. If you do this often enough, the replacement process of thought/feeling will happen automatically. What will now happen, as a result, is the inability of a bad situation from effecting your energy level. You will be able to hold and gather your energy and as such be able to re-utilize it for another more valuable and significant purpose. Do not forget that each of us has only a fixed amount of energy to use in a day and the more energy used up in anger, hatred, argument and bad feeling, the less energy becomes available for anything else worthwhile which you would like to do. In closing, Life is nothing but an Energy game, the  more energy you store and/or gather, the stronger you become and the easier it is for you to accomplish your goals.

The perception of personal rejection in a private or business relationship is a great waster of Energy and prevents you from focusing on what you need to do consistently to win and achieve in your daily Life activity. Learn to combine positive thinking as a counteraction to negative rejection feelings and you will not only do better in all your activities but will also feel more happier and harmonious in your affairs.

## POSITIVISM AND FLEXIBILITY

Flexibility is the capacity to make changes in your Life journey. And Life does throw you a curve now and then. It is how you accept this curve and navigate further which makes the difference between failure and success. Let us best illustrate this example by way of a short story. A salesperson tries to hit his annual sales goal but finds midway through the process that his manager has got fired and a new one appointed who provides him with a lack of direction. How must he adjust to this situation? By being pissed off at his company, by adopting a negative attitude towards his new manager, by getting mad at himself for having chosen this sales organization? This is a classic example of the challenging need for flexibility. The salesperson needs to continue his focus on his annual goal knowing that no one is going to help him achieve it as much as he himself. He must be flexible by accepting and adjusting to the new management change, never losing focus of his goal. He should also work creatively to enlist the cooperation of his new manager in the achievement of his sales goals.

Flexibility means accepting Life's situations as and when they present themselves. It means knowing that irrespective of what happens on the outside to deter or distract you, that you will remain steadfast to your intention to achieve. A great challenge in achieving mental flexibility is being able to be aware of negative emotion as and when it arises and having the courage to be able to ignore this negativity. Disallowing this negativity to enter your Life by not stroking the negative thoughts as they develop into strong feelings and then into a strong negative outwardly action is critical here. It is at this juncture that Positive thinking helps.

Positive thinking must be reinforced as an invigorator and a guide towards the achievement of a goal in all circumstances both good and bad. Positive thinking assisted with a flexible Life approach does wonders in helping you maintain your mental and emotional balance as you fire ahead to win your prize---- to reach your station in Life where you are fulfilled.

## POSITIVISM AND LIVING NATURALLY

Natural living assumes a simplistic approach to Life. It means being composed and relaxed in everything you do. Like Nature, which has a living code, you must attempt to blend your mental and emotional activities so they merge with natural order. And what is a natural order? It is a way of behaving with others and working cooperatively to achieve a goal. Early on, you must realize that you need the cooperation of others to reach your goal and that your primary concern should be in helping others to get where they want to go, knowing very well in your heart that helping these others will generate your own reward. Natural living means having the capacity to understand that all Living is interrelated as you strive to build a better Life for yourself. You must as a natural rule, help others to reach their own destination now. Therefore, your work does not call for manipulating others to meet with your personal selfish objectives but looks at your contribution to the world as the first step to achieving your own station in Life. This calls for a win-win cooperative situation whether it be in a job or your own small business.

Natural living also entails spending time in quietness and peace with yourself and in quiet contemplation. It means having a positive attitude and relationship with other people, with Nature and with your own thoughts and feelings towards objects and your ideas. This type of living is a way of Life, which operates in the background. Positive attitudes in these various relationships supports your success and helps provide the much needed positive energy to achieve your goals.

## POSITIVISM AND LIVING WITHOUT EXCESS

In most of the books on Positive Thinking and Goal Achievement, there seems to be a common strand of thought, which goes somewhat like this: "Life is about Success, which involves the achievement of a predetermined goal." Although I have no bones to pick with this saying, which is true in many respects, I wonder why it is not important to discuss what is this desire you want to fulfill. Does fulfillment of a specific random urge justify the means one uses to achieve it? At the risk of getting a little philosophical, I challenge every reader to give this thought more attention. And as we stop to ponder about the importance of fulfilling one or more desires, I start thinking of how many individuals feel gratified by achieving a pre-determined Life of Excess.

This Life of Excess is not something which is inherent in our Nature, but is taught to us by our culture, peer group and social networks. All the advertising pressure, the movies, the internet among other media, reek of this. The lamentations say that a person must have as a minimum goals like, "Get rich quick, spend a lot of money, travel incessantly, have numerous sexual liaisons, rob, cheat and steal without getting caught but eventually get what you want." It appears when you watch a movie or read an article that getting rich at any cost is permissible by Society. And that once you get rich, you should spend like crazy--- buy boats, big mansions, have many girlfriends; this qualifies you in belonging to this exclusive club of wealthy people. And, therefore, the goals you put in place seem to want to satisfy this brainwashed urge from the outside.

One must ask oneself rather seriously if this is consciously or sub-consciously the Life of Excess you have chosen or whether you want a Life more tuned to your own special and unique needs, wishes and desires. And if it is the latter, how do you tune out all the negative brainwashing images and messages you deal with every day? Positive thinking helps you to fortify your own special goals and objectives by repetition. Constant repetition helps you stay on your path, while ignoring the demands of advertisers, social media and cultural pressures.

On the other hand, one must question how much desire needs to be fulfilled for a person to feel he has reached a happy station in Life. After attaining an acceptable amount of food, water, shelter, sex and a feeling of belonging, how much more of desire needs to be fulfilled? Where is the balance between outer success and inner peace and happiness? And where is the trade off point for you? How much energy are you prepared to commit to external growth ventures leading to material and professional success? And how much time and energy do you want to spend with friends and family? And what about the time required for your personal growth? And for growth within your spiritual Life?

These are tough and difficult decisions and only you can make the right decision for yourself. Suffice to say, these considerations must be taken into hand when charting your personal Life plan. It is not about just material success. It is about living Life wholly from the inside out, serving others while achieving your goals. It is about philanthropy and kindness to others weaker than you mentally and emotionally.

A proper balanced Life marks time for all the activities important for your growth and self-development. It takes into account you peculiar needs and wants. It also takes into account your natural talent and abilities and defines what turns you on in your career development and your personal Life. Only a proper balance can assist you live a happy, harmonious Life. And is that not what we all consciously and subconsciously strive for--- a Life of fulfillment and happiness – a life filled with much love and harmony while doing what we enjoy most????????

Living without excess is the first step in opening up your personal door to fulfillment.

## POSITIVISM AND GREATNESS

Greatness is a remarkable quality expressed by a few. Leaders of the world like Mahatma Gandhi believed in liberation of his people from the foreign oppressors who victimized and exploited Indian soil for over two centuries. His thoughts, feelings and actions inspired and motivated a country locked into slavery to rise up and face the oppressors. And he was able to evict the aggressors from Indian soil without raising a gun or engaging in any form of violence. His non-violence movement became a symbol for all of Mankind where goals for the good of others could be achieved without violence and bloodshed.

Another great world leader was Martin Luther King. Dr. King believed in the concept of equality and justice for all. He was most unhappy to see the conditions of blacks in the United States. He wanted to uplift them from their misery by granting them equal opportunity with all others in the land. He met with tremendous resistance in his struggle and finally had to pay for his beliefs by being assassinated. But his thoughts and ideals led to positive fruits as blacks were granted more rights and more freedom of opportunity.

Can you visualize yourself making a contribution to the world like Gandhi or Martin Luther King? Perhaps not. But does this matter??? You do have the opportunity to emulate these individuals or any others whose values and actions you revere. Greatness is something you can aspire to in your own special way. Even if you may not be another Gandhi or Dr. King you can work towards being the best in your field. In that respect, you can express greatness. To me, greatness means helping others quintessentially. And if you can do that in whatever station in Life you hold, then you, too have expressed your greatness and contributed to the betterment of Mankind.

How does Positive Thinking work with greatness? By constant reminder and use, positive thinking challenges you to higher and higher levels of performance and service to others. Your definition of greatness now involves not only reaching your goal but also helping others reach their goal. Your outstanding service to others is a mark of greatness, since your contribution is felt, acknowledged and accepted by another. Positive thinking works with greatness to enhance your reputation and to motivate you to do more and more for others, some of whom may be disadvantaged or weaker than you mentally or emotionally.

When all is said and done, the mark of a great man is not only his worldly success in reaching his goal, but his ability to help others. If you contribute through your actions in your working Life and, in addition donate philanthropically after your death, what greater Service can you provide to Mankind?

I would like to end this section by talking about a charitable hospital in India where diagnostic and surgical services are provided free of charge to many poor people. And when I walk into this hospital, I see the picture of the main donor who donated hundreds of thousands of rupees to the uplifment of this hospital. When I look at the photograph of this man, which adorns the front of the hospital, I simply cannot help but look into the eyes of this generous donor---- eyes which are kind and helpful, which represent a heart full of love and mercy. Here is a rich man, who cared deeply for the medical needs of the very poor, who could not afford treatment. He not only took care of his family's needs but created the seeds of a philanthropic revolution in this hospital-----what greater way than this exists to contribute to others? He started a stream of new donors who now generously contribute to the hospital fund to finance operations, treatments and diagnosis for the benefit of the very poor.

# POSITIVISM AND LIVING CALMLY

Living calmly is a rare virtue found in a very few. By calm living, I mean a non- reactive Lifestyle. Most of us get upset and irritated when Life does not hand us what we wish and desire. The emotions boil negatively to the surface and the resistance to what we see as our present Life result is strong-----it results in anger, disappointment, frustration, jealousy and depression.

A peaceful inner Life is one which is devoid of negative emotion. But ain't it hard to stay at an even level emotionally when things don't go our way. Stress is well known in North America to have killed hundreds of thousands of people. Some people are not happy because they are not rich, some because their spouses or girlfriends have left them and some due to a family problem. We seem to encounter so many problems as we graduate towards Life's situations. Life in its very nature involves change. And we humans are very slow at adjusting to change, particularly when that change is not something we want or feel we need. The strong negative emotions, ruin our peace of mind and get us agitated and even insomniac in some conditions. At this stage in our Life, living calmly becomes only a pipe dream, something we read in a book and nothing close to our Real Life.

How does one live calmly? By focusing on what the gain-able positive benefits are of this way of Life. Positive benefits include longevity, better Life, more Energy to enjoy and better relationships with our loved ones. It also involves growing into spirituality and having a more positive relationship with everyone around us. In order to start moving towards a life of calmness, one needs to examine the positive benefits of such a Life and then through an understanding of this, an attempt to self motivate yourself to mind your thoughts, feelings and actions so you express everything in great calmness and ease.

How does Positive Thinking help in this mission of calmness? By focusing on the value and benefits of calmness and by encouraging you to stay active and alert inward to see signs of outer mental and emotional strain and to steer you back to a life which though active and energetic remains centered in the inside with great calmness and love. Positive thinking holds this image of calmness and peace at all times, both good and turbulent and acts as your guide to a more balanced and happy Lifestyle.

## POSITIVISM AND LIVING BEYOND APPEARANCES

We live in a social setup, which judges us on the way we dress, the way we look, the car we drive and the house we live in, among other things. To so many, this external appearance marks the pinnacle of image creation----- we tend to impress and wow others by mere physical factors.

However, unknown to many, there are mysterious energy centers working in the background. Have you been to a party and suddenly seen someone you have never known before, who instantly appeals to your sense and sensibility? And this person has not even opened his mouth or uttered a word of any kind. What has happened here is that his Inner Energy has pierced the social environment and touched you. Here is possibly a person, who lives beyond appearances.

When your inner and outer purpose are aligned you create a very powerful energy field----your inner love, peace and harmony are expressed to the world at large and touches everything and everyone you come in contact with. Here is a true expression of a Life lived in dedication to your core values. Obviously you must ask yourself if this way of Living makes sense to you. Or would you like to appear like an egotistical self-confident person, who projects he knows everything and has acquired a superior material station in Life? Although there is nothing wrong in being as successful as you want to be materially, you do have a choice in how you express this Success. It has always been my belief and opinion that all success starts with inner alignment and Success and if a person's inner values are one of love, peace and service to others that these qualities will create an outer success in time. The combination of these two factors, the inner appearance (of peace and harmony) combine with an outer expression/appearance (of outer order) will result in the best possible result for this person and more important to the people who this person comes in contact with.

And how does Positivism come into this equation? By challenging you to constantly focus on the positive inner qualities you aspire to cultivate and express. And to combine with with external positivism in achieving your written and valuable (external) goals. You now remember it is not all about external appearances but truly about building and developing your inner appearance. The power, the glory, the success and happiness is in focusing on inner qualities. Only with this focus can you truly be both successful in whatever you want, not forgetting that part of your offering to the World is the process of assisting others to getting to where they want to go.

## POSITIVISM AND LIVING BEYOND SUPERFICIALITY

Living superficially is a common way of existence of many. We have this projection of the ideal life of the Jones-es family. This family image has got indelibly ingrained in our collective memory. A two income family living in the suburbs with 1.5 children(1 kid and a dog), two cars, two paid vacations a year and plenty for all. And so many lives are wasted only in the process of seeking what others think is best for us. Superficiality means living up to someone else's expectations---- the story above is just a case in point. It means having to look at every turn and corner in Life hoping to see a sign of acceptance from others and then molding your Life and Energy to suit others. What a waste of a life.

Living beyond superficiality is living a Life without boundaries; a Life blessed with what you truly wish. And the courage to take risks to find your special place in the sun. In this process one lives through volatility and change as one attempts to bend the universe to meet one's Life expectation. This is working with the Law of Attraction to the extreme.

A life without superficiality is a happy Life; it is a Life uniquely private to your needs and concerns. This is Living with grace, without worry or anxiety for tomorrow, knowing that the Universal Energy will always provide. It means being impervious to criticism or other negative comments from others including the ones you love and respect. Such a Life is marked with simplicity, grace and Happiness.

And how does Positive Thinking help in achieving this state of Life? By constantly repeating to yourself mentally the positive benefits of the path you have chosen, by constantly stroking yourself mentally and emotionally through Affirmation that this Life will turn out exactly as you wish. That you deserve greatness and happiness. And that all good things will come to pass.

# POSITIVISM AND LIVING BEYOND JUDGMENT

Judgment is often employed by humans to cast others in a more negative light. It seems that many humans feel more privileged to have a better Life than others and therefore look down on the poorer misfits. Such an attitude pervades most World Societies, and causes irreparable emotional damage to others. I have been in poor tenements and slum areas in India where people have lost all hope of Life, where they are the constant victims of mental torture from the richer sections of society. And where will this end?????

Everything good and bad starts with one person. And so it is with Societies and relationships between people. If one needs to change a Societal way of thinking, then one can only start with oneself. The first thing is to realize the devastating, negative effect of judging others negatively. Criticizing others while extolling your virtues is the worst way to be. If you understand this is not the way you want your Life to go, then you open a door to starting to make the first step to living a Life non judgmentally.

A life without judgment is an attitude that everyone has a right to be. Everyone has got to their station in Life by things they have done or not done properly. Also, in emerging nations where poverty is rooted, several million people have just been born in poverty. And these things exist and time must pass as people evolve and self determine their future. This wave is already upon India where the economic growth is creating better economic futures for numerous poor people.

And as you do not judge others, then it follows by a natural law that less people will judge you. When you get judged, you just smile and let the thought and feeling pass in terms of judgment by others. That is their opinion of your Life and not yours; you are happy just the way you are, whether super rich or rich or simple. Live your Life the way you feel most happy and all good things will happen to you.

Positive thought supports the contention that all Life is valuable and that you have a right to apply your positive thought in the direction of your choice without violating the rights and opportunities of others. Living life without judgment opens up a positive pathway to much peace, harmony and self fulfillment. Live and let live should be everyone's motto as we share this space we call Earth to help each other grow and become better humans in every way.

# POSITIVISM AND LIVING HONORABLY

Living honorably involves an existence marked with grace and simplicity. And it is also includes a Life in positive service to others, knowing that we are all interlinked together in one common Universe. It involves having a reverence to Life and all things in it. To detail further, an honorable Life is one lived in calmness and peace, where all achievement is made in strict cooperation with others and in a spirit of mutual benefit. Thinking, speaking and action are all coordinated and comprehensive with no room for conflict. The energy created through this way of Life is magnetic, powerful and of great positive influence in the World.

Why should one live an honorable Life? Because this is the only Life which is sustainable Survival wise on this Planet we call Mother Earth, on a long term basis. When you note what is happening in the world with every human being scrambling for a few more crumbs of money and space, it is rare to find someone who is not only happy with the direction in which he is going but also a person who sees no conflict between his needs and wants and other people's requirements for an honorable Life, too. And as you scan the environment, you see the result of most people's Life--- a Life marked with extreme strife, jealousy, anger and hatred. And then the final evolution of this approach, which is violence and war. We have seen the effect of War as it has killed hundreds of thousands of people. The change needs to come with a few people first, which will then expand to cover more. This spiritual change has already started, where people in different parts of the world have started exploring living in a new way.

And how does Positive thinking assist in culmination of this honorable Life? By keeping in mind, foremost that we humans are all connected and the key to the good and happy Life is to think, talk and act positive all the time. To choose to look at the good things in people and ignore the bad aspects. To focus the mind on the positive aspects of achievement, while negating the anger, hatred and violence. By waking up every day with a fresh and happy smile, looking forward to tackling the days challenges. And above all, to know, that there is a Universal Energy behind you supporting your positive thought and attitude.

## POSITIVISM AND LIVING AS IF YOUR LIFE MAKES A DIFFERENCE

Your Life is very precious, not only to you but to the world in general. Your actions combined with the action of other humans creates and influences the World environment. As such, each human has the responsibility to make the world more positive, happy and thus contribute quintessentially to make a real difference.

Some cumulative effects of human action have created deleterious effects. Environmental degradation, global warming, regional wars and confrontations, poverty and inequality are all key indicators of a Life of waste and negativism. Therefore, your actions and relationships on a global scale are creating a positive or negative effect.

If you accept the notion that your Life is precious, then you will take steps to improving its content. You can do this by learning new things, by responding more positively to others, by accentuating your level of service to humanity and in being the best you can be in your chosen field. A life of difference means that you live in eternal Mindfulness, that you live with complete awareness of your surroundings and your relationship with people, nature and things around you. You are also very aware of the results you are creating through your actions and strive to improve the quality of your Life.

Positive thinking helps you stay on track with this Life mission of excellence. Since you understand and accept how important every second of your Life is, you focus on staying positive all the time. When negative thoughts arise, you recognize them but do not expand on them. This way your inner space is permeated by a wave of positivism, which when combined with your overall purpose in Life and your very own private goals helps you become more effective and efficient in everything you touch and do. And not to forget, this application of Positivism is essential to creation and sustenance of a more happy and fulfilled Life.

## POSITIVISM AND LETTING GO OF THE FINAL RESULT

In one of the holiest books of the Hindus, "the Bhagvad Gita", Lord Krishna explains to the warrior price Arjuna, that he must fight the battle at Kuruskhetra with an attitude of letting go of the final result. This is a remarkable but true expression of wisdom. The great Arjuna is hesitant about going to war with his family cousins in the battlefield. Lord Krishna in a vision to Arjuna mentions that this is a war being waged against greed, dishonesty and corruption and that although these relatives are part of his family, he must do whatever he can to fight injustice and in the process restore. Peace and Order in the Kingdom. Lord Krishna teaches Arjuna not to focus on the end result of the war but to fight it now with his full power knowing well that in the end, truth and justice will prevail. Through this vision, Arjuna is brought to gather the courage and confidence required to fight this bloody battle and vanquish the intolerant and unjust relatives.

For most of us, letting go of the final result seems impossible. In the Western culture, we are so much focused on end results, that if it takes a little longer to achieve this end result, we panic or alternatively become impatient, angry and frustrated. We seem to accept the cultural brainwashing that instant effort must equal instant results. But such is not the way of Life. Sometimes, good results take a long time to express themselves and if one does not stay focused on the course, the results become very negative. Very simply, to achieve any Life result one not only needs a clear goal with a time deadline, but honest and hard work to make that dream come true. Sometimes, when the deadline passes and the result is still not clearly in hand, one can get despondent and unhappy knowing that you have done everything in your power to achieve your result. If one looks closely, one must realize that the environment does not always throw out positive results the way you may want it, time-wise. Sometimes, you need to reset the goal or look deeply into what hidden obstacles are there in your path. Sometimes these obstacles are self imposed but hidden at a subconscious level; sometimes the environmental obstacles appear insurmountable. The person who is the most successful is the one who understands the race goes to the tortoise and not to the hare. Slow and consistent progress, even if this means not hitting your goals all the time, will eventually lead to great long term success as compared to you just being a flash in the pan, earning short term results but not achieving much long term. It is like winning a Life battle but losing the War.

Now let me go one step further to clarify the teaching in the Bhagvad Gita of letting go of the result. This teaching is highly advanced and when adapted to Western conditions means that after you set your goal and the time deadline to achieve it, you release the notion of final result. That is, you just shut your eyes, roll up your sleeves and work hard, not worrying about when or if you will reach your self assigned goal. You instead, trust your capacity and the Universal energy around you to assist you in your endeavor. It is as if an invisible Hand will lead you forward to your Mecca. And while you are experiencing this attitude you positively visualize that you have already received the fruits of your hard work. This is negating the usual rationality of the Mind and sending out thanks to the Universe for giving you what you deserve. Please note you are doing this in advance, accompanied with the utmost Faith in your endeavor. And this faith is accompanied by your unconditional Spirit of Allowing that newness to occur in your Life. If you really look at this deeply, that is all you can really do. Stay positive, think positive and act positive in the direction of your dream. Reinforce the positivity by constant visualization, by gratitude for your gift to be received in advance and a total opening of your heart center with the gift of allowance, which keeps your energy channels open to the newness which is going to happen. And also, importantly, a complete conscious rejection of any negative thoughts, or self doubt and fear which is likely to express itself when you are in this path to reaching your very special goal.

Positive thinking now becomes a much needed ally in assisting you crystallize your goal in material space. A reverence for Positive thinking, a total dedication to its practice and a simple and trusting heart will all assist in giving you what you need and wish for.

## POSITIVISM AND LIVING UNTROUBLED BY GOOD OR BAD FORTUNE

Life, for most humans, is marked with periods of great fortune interspersed with indifferent wealth accumulation periods. And there is also the presence of bad fortune. By fortune, I mean more than wealth accumulation. Since real riches are measured by the quantum of happiness experienced by a human, it is very rare to set up a publicly measurable comparative scale. However, real wealth can be visualized as the summation of good health, good relationships, economic wealth and service to others. So, for the rest of this chapter, please understand this is the definition with which I write about this subject.

Every human being has the remarkable capacity of knowing how his Life is expressing itself, the level of happiness, relationship and other wealth factors. This cumulative result is then expressed through the mechanism of the sub conscious into the conscious level. Have you sometimes, felt really high about your Life, when things are really going well and the Universe is cooperating with you? And at other times in your Life have you experienced a down feeling when nothing seems to be going right?

The key to Positive Living is to accept both ups and downs in Life simultaneously with the same zest and vigor. What I mean is that one first has to understand the material nature of Life, which is extremely volatile and ever changing. Nothing is and nothing will ever stay the same. The only constant in this world is change. If you always want to be high, you are in for a deep and disturbing awakening. Nature will not cooperate with you.

The key to a successful Life is enjoying all your highs to the fullest, but also with a spirit of humility and reverence accepting the bad things happening to you in your environment. By accepting I do not mean that you try not to change your circumstance but the mere acceptance of the fact that something bad has happened. And the faith and wisdom that this too will pass. If you can keep yourself positive through difficult times, then the extra mental and emotional energy generated by not being unhappy, stressed, angry or despondent will help you overcome this negative situation quickly. How does this extra mental and emotional energy get generated? Very simply, we all have a quantum of energy available to us for distribution in a daily basis. There may be slight variations in this quantum, but for most practical purpose there is a well defined human range of energy available.

If you are angry or stressed, a pool of energy is sucked out of your human daily energy potential and diverted to mental and emotional activities causing pain, like anger, jealousy and depression. The key is to lessen the flow of energy into these negative centers. If you accept that something bad has happened, you slow down this diversion of energy. If you further proceed to look at this situation positively, trying to learn from the calamity, you further slow down this diversion of energy. If simultaneously you practice Faith and Prayer, asking the Universal Energy to guide you through this calamity you will find you move out of the Negative to the Positive very quickly.

Positive thinking helps you understand that there is good and bad fortune in everyone's Life. Some people are blessed with more good fortune and others are cursed with more bad fortune. But this does not mean that anyone is better or worse than you. You need to focus on your Life and your goals and wishes. You are unique in every way possible, and your challenge is to stay positive in good times and bad, so that you can harness the universal power to convert negative experiences and results into positive ones in the quickest possible time. And you will find that this approach will result in more calmness, balance and harmony in your Life. Happiness and a deeper sense of contentment will follow this process.

## POSITIVISM AND LIVING WITH NO FEAR OF DEATH

The fear of death is an intense, negative emotion. And, in so many cases, this is not experienced on a conscious level, but on a highly sub-conscious plane. Events triggered in your Life cause you to experience the pain resulting from this fear of death. Some common Life triggers causing exposure to this fear are:

*Death of someone close.*

*Death of a family member.*

*Sudden exposure to a life threatening disease like cancer, stroke, etc.*

*Death resulting from an accident involving a close friend or family member.*

The exposure to a death experience causes one to remember his mortality. And, if this negative experience is turned around positively, one then realizes how precious each and every moment is. Many new age Western thinkers have proclaimed in North America that one must life every moment as if it is his last, but do we really take heed of this advise?

When I was attending sales school, a motivation speaker who was invited to our office challenged the salespeople with the following question, "If this was the last year of your Life, what would you do? How would you live your Life? Would it be any different than the way you are living now?" These questions disturbed me as a young sales professional and forced me to reevaluate some of my goals in terms of understanding and acting my Life in the moment. I now incorporated new goals in my annual goal book and tried harder to balance my Life with a combination of work and play.

Positivism can be employed in changing your attitude so you live every moment as if it is your last. This necessarily means that you now have an incentive to be more positive as you sense the urgency of Life. If you truly have no fear of death and can turn around this negative thought, then one can live a better, happier and more decisive Life. You can then overcome one of the major mortal fears and convert it into a highly positive basis for Living. For what is more important, living now or fearing for your Future tomorrow? One is real and available to you now, the other is an intangible unknown projection, which has the power to create negativity through the medium of fear? The choice seems simple and straightforward: Live Life now and to the fullest based on all your God given talents and positivism. And results will flow in your favor.

## POSITIVISM AND OFFERING SURPLUS

Offering surplus is an important Act of life and one which is always recognized by the Universe. Offering surplus means giving some of the fruits of your hard work to charity. It also means going out of your way to helping others in need of advice. It means placing other people's interests over yours.

An insurance sales adviser I new did the most remarkable thing I have seen, given his economic and financial situation. Here was a man with a family and few children with great responsibilities-----however he chose to give to charity a sum of 25% of his gross income every month. When I first met him, I was surprised at this benevolent act. How could such a man give to charity first before he fed his family and took care of his personal and business needs? One day over coffee, I tried to understand his philosophy. And he told me his remarkable story. He said that in the beginning the charitable act was frightening because as a new insurance adviser with earnings based on commissions, he did not know if would have enough money to feed his family and have anything left over to charity. But he was a deeply religious man and committed to his community and said that in spite of all his fears and misgivings he decided to go ahead with this project. What happened afterward is a story surrounding effects stemming from the miracle of giving. He found that every time he gave, his income was miraculously increased. Now this was very difficult for a young mind like mine to grasp rationally. So I abandoned my rationality to understand his true Life story.  And this brings me to the Law of Surplus. This Law says that if you give a part of what you earn to others, then you will get more in return. When I asked this adviser if this law held any value in his Life, he said it did. However, he pointed it out to me that this was not his motivation to give. His religious motivation was to help others and if he got something back from the Universe to reward him for his gracious act then he would accept it. And he accepted gracefully the fact that as he gave, his financial practice grew, his income quadrupled in a few years and he had a better Life for himself and his family. I cannot think of a better way of illustrating this Law of Surplus.

Positive thinking can be a partner in the practice of the Law of Surplus. Positive thinking can guide you to understand that you must offer something to others who are weaker and less successful than you . This Positive Act of Charity is offered with the utmost Faith and with no agenda to receive more in in return. It is simply giving for the sake of giving.

# POSITIVISM AND LIVING WITHOUT RESENTMENT

Resentment is one of those things, which burns a hole in the character of Man. The causes of resentment are too many to mention. Some of the causes could include an inability to get what you want, a failed personal relationship, constant argument with others and other personality disorders. It really does not matter where the resentment comes from---- what is important is to understand and accept that resentment is a major energy distraction. It pulls out a great deal of Energy from your daily Energy bank and leaves you with so little energy to do all the other things you want to do.

Resentment also carries forward into existing and new relationships. With resentment you are always finding fault with your partner, your boss, your co- workers and with strangers. Resentment breeds an air of animosity and confrontation, both of which are really difficult qualities to interact with others. So knowing that, how do you reverse Resentment?

The best and most effective way is to do it through the Practice of Meditation. If you can sit quietly in a place for a short period of time and focus on this resentment, you will be able to see which thoughts and feelings of resentment get associated with specific past Life experiences. So, if you find that a broken love affair is the primary focus point of this resentment, then you need to go into this broken relationship and see how and why this is effecting you today. In many cases, the simple awareness of the major causes for resentment will cure you of its bad effects. In another case, if you just feel listless and depressed and cannot pinpoint the cause of resentment, you need to work harder on your self observation and meditation. If you stay in meditative mode for long enough you will find the cause of this depression and once the cause is found, you can work on overcoming the negative effects of resentment.

Positive thinking becomes a light which assists you in both moving forward and in being aware of negative feelings like resentment in your framework. Positive thinking brings forth the hope that you can lick all the issues involving resentment though proper understanding of its underlying emotional causes. It also serves as a constant brake to stop you from fueling the resentment by thinking further negative thoughts. Positive or negative? Positive equals happiness and negative equals depression. Which way do you want to go?

By exercising your right to 100% positivism all the time, every day and every second of your Life you are now putting into effect a new consciousness cycle which will get rid of your resentment and put you towards a path of happiness and self fulfillment.

## POSITIVISM AND LIVING WITHOUT ATTACHMENT

Attachment is a common human condition. As we acquire things and experiences, both materially and non-materially, we tend to not only be attracted to these new found gifts, but also envelop our identity around them. Let me provide a small example. A young man out of graduate school has finally married his childhood sweetheart. He works hard for many years to collect a down payment for a house in the suburbs and he now lives happily there with his wife, a dog and one kid. He is doing well at his job. And everything is going well. Till a tragedy occurs. He has been fired from his job. And his Life comes stumbling down. His identity now comprises his well paying job, his house, his relationship with his wife, etcetera and when one of them is lost he is frustrated and tense. A common human reaction? You bet. An acceptable reaction to a job loss? Yes and No. I would say, "Yes," on a short term basis since everyone normally reacts negatively to a job loss and immediate loss of income. But I would say, " No," to a long term approach to this issue.  And this brings be back to the subject of attachment. As Life went well for this young fella, he acquired a sense of security to all his worldly belongings and established relationships. And there grew a sense of attachment to these wonderful things. He associated his life with them since he chose to identify with them. And attachment slipped in between the cracks at some points. He was so attached to all his wonderful things that the loss of one of them triggered a massive reaction.

What I would like to talk to you about is not the usual loss of one or more things we cherish. Nor do I want to provide a sermon of why you should  not be attached to what you love. I want to instead talk about how much more beautiful Life would be if you lived it without attachment. Which means you can still enjoy your car, your house, your dog and all your wonderful relationships, knowing that nothing will last forever. North American relationships are another case in point. It is a well documented fact that about half of all marriages in North America land up in divorce. So, to fortify what I am trying to say is that if one entered the institution of marriage with a spirit of humility and adjustment and gave it the best one could give, one would not be that much bothered long term if it failed. Is this possible? Maybe it is not for you. The point I am trying to make in a very round about fashion, is that it is possible to live and love without attachment, it is possible to attract wealth and love in your Life now.

However not knowing or caring about the final game result is always best. It will give you the power to work more harder on your relationship; it will give you the strength to endure more financial and personal storms and in the end it will give you the power to live life moment to moment. The more attachment you have to your desire, the harder it is to live a complete and full Life without suffering.

Lord Gautama Buddha, the founder of the movement of Buddhism, declared in one of his speeches after enlightenment that the root cause of suffering and pain in this world was desire and attachment to the objects of desire. If you want to truly be happy, then go after your dream and achieve your purpose knowing fully that nothing lasts forever and that you are on a trip and this trip must end. Is it possible to enjoy something with your full Mind, your full Heart, your full being without being attached to this possession, thought, pleasure and experience? That is a challenge I throw up to you readers who are looking for a better angle to your Life.

Positive thinking focuses on the present moment and therefore, if applied properly cuts the chord between your past and future. Although you have future goals, you realize you need to attain it in the present moment. So, you attempt to break away from the chains of attachment and just do everything you can at this moment to realize your Life----- nothing more and nothing Else.

## POSITIVISM AND LIVING WITH YOUR INNER LIGHT

Your inner light must remain your guiding force in your life. And what do I refer to as inner light? Let me first explain what it is not. It is not your rational thought or your emotional signals, nor is it your physical predisposition. Your inner light is the wisdom derived from intuitive expression.

Intuitive expression resides in the deepest layers of your Self and transcends the boundaries of your conscious and sub conscious mind. It is contact at a very deep level beyond the subconscious. This layer of consciousness can be realized through meditation and other similar practices. Intuitive understanding is a flash of intelligence with no cause, with no beginning and end. It is a flash of light which signals you in a certain direction. We, as humans, all experience this special moment when we get a flash from the hidden realms of our consciousness, which beckons us to act in a certain way. And many of us, follow this flash of intuition.

Living with the inner light means cultivating the surrounding and environment to invite this light into your Life. The less mind, heart and body focused you become, the more detached you are and in this process of quietness and detachment you are able to tap into this mysterious energy. Many humans, in time of great adversity, sit quietly and ponder about their next plan of action and often a mysterious inner voice beckons to them guiding them along a certain direction. But there are those who reject these intuitive flashes, instead choosing to rely on their rational or emotional experience to guide them elsewhere.

In my view, living a Life blessed with the Inner Light is the only real purpose of Life. Life must be lived from the inside out and not from the outside in. Most people get bombarded with numerous changes in their external environment and are constantly acting and reacting to external change. Their Life become a never changing procession of relationships and impact of same. Why not live a life from the inside out? Which means you still go out and about your Life as you are now except you do it with a different understanding and wisdom. This wisdom allows you to see the temporal nature of all things material and the volatility of external relationships. You view these connections as important but temporary. You then focus more on your inner journey to a place of more peace and happiness. In this way, you live more in simplicity and with your intuitive urges and less on external reaction. While you react to external events, you do so in a more quiet and happy manner knowing that these effects do not define you.

Your house, your car, your job do not define you. You are much more vital and significant than these things. And this discovery leads to a new and different way of Life, where you are inwardly happy and express and touch everything outside with the same level of positivism and energy.

Positive thinking offers hope that a new World and a new way of thinking are not only possible but within your grasp. This thinking provides you with the best way of interacting with others on your worldly plans but still keeps your energy bank intact to do other vital things like understanding the universe, understanding yourself and your relationship to the Universe and gives you the pathway to create a new level of consciousness.

I would like to end this chapter with a saying from a great saint and spiritual teacher from India, Ramana Maharishi, who said that before you go on any spiritual adventure, you must first ask yourself, "Who am I,? "And only after you discover the right answer to this question  can you attempt to find a better and more significant Life for yourself---- a Life filled with Love, Positivism and much grace.

# POSITIVISM AND GOAL SETTING

Goal setting is an important starting point, which leads to the achievement of your material goals and dreams. Many times one wants something bad enough but fails to focus on this goal. For example, if you want to buy and live in a nice home, it may be something you desire, however you do not crystallize this desire and as a result do not attain what you want. Goal setting is the first stage in human achievement.

So if owning a house is a major dream for you, why not pen this desire down in writing? Research has shown that putting down your dreams in writing gives it a particularly strong force. By writing it down, you have shown an initiative of committing to your desire. It also now becomes quite tangible as it is expressed in physical form. It is also something, which you can refer to again and again and therefore becomes a repetitive source of personal motivation. The second aspect of goal setting is to set a deadline. So, if you wanted a nice home and knew what it would look like but did not set a deadline, then it would take you a longer time to attract that home into your Life. When you say, " I want a 4 bedroom house in the suburbs by ---------( 2 years from now), you are setting up a very powerful course of future Attraction. You are now committed to attracting what you wish from the Universe within a well defined range of time. The time deadline must always be specific, in terms of the exact day, date and year. This will help acceleration of your goal achievement.

To accentuate the results flowing from good goal setting, I would encourage you to get a picture of a sample house from a local builder or draw a picture of an ideal house with bedrooms, bathrooms, living room, garden in perfect details and paste this picture in front of your car dashboard, in your office table, in your bathroom mirror, in your bedroom mirror so you can see clearly the object of your desire. The more you stroke yourself positively, the easier will that arrive in your Life.

Positive thinking supports the goal setting process. It gives you the added confidence of crystallizing and reinforcing your goals. It further allows you to focus on the mental and physical pictures you generate to help you achieve your goal faster.

# POSITIVISM AND A PLAN OF ACTION

Your Plan of Personal Action is an important part of your blueprint to Success. You have now crystallized your goals, you have committed them to writing, you have set a time deadline to achieve them. You have further drawn mental pictures of the goal, like the kind of house you want. Can you just stop here and allow Nature to do its work? That is ridiculous. You have to sow the seeds of hard work through positive action to attract what you wish for.

Your personal plan of Action is a step by step action process which steers you towards accomplishment of your goal---- therefore, if you want to buy a house and need to accumulate a certain amount of dawn payment and want the home in two years, you need to save, say 24000 dollars in 24 months, i.e. 1000 dollars per month. Your plan of action now includes a subsidiary plan of savings, which generates an additional 1000 dollars per month which gets directed into a savings account for you to reach your objective. The next aspect of your planning is to find out ways and means of generating that 1000 dollar savings very month. Can you accomplish this on your current income? Will you need to moonlight to generate additional income? Will you need to find another job with better income opportunity? Once these decisions are made, then you need to monitor your plan of action. Are you on track to reach your accumulation goal cumulatively? So, st the end of three months do you have 3000 dollars in your savings account? If not, what can you do to increased your savings in the next three months?

Positive thinking gives you the courage to dream big. Positive thinking assists in visualizing the end outcome of a beautiful house with the 25000 dollars in hand as a down payment. Positive attitude helps you to constantly monitor your plan of action knowing that you will achieve your final goal to get your dream house within the time period you have allocated.

# POSITIVISM AND STRATEGIZING YOUR LIFE PORTFOLIO

The word, portfolio, is usually associated with a financial and investment plan. In the traditional understanding of the word portfolio, as sit relates to financial engineering, it is viewed as a way of viewing all your investments as a whole and not in separate compartments. For example, an investor wants to make money and looks at a specific investment which may return him, say, 10 per cent approximately, in the first year. He makes this investment in addition to another investments and still may find at the end of the year that he has lost money as a whole. This brings the concept of portfolio planning where you merge all your investments into one whole and look at your wealth performance as a combination and interaction of results of varying components of your portfolio and then look at everything as a whole.

Looking at the above as a perfect example, one now sees that Life too must be viewed as a strategic whole. It is not good enough to say you are rich or satisfied with one area on your Life but to view the performance of the entire whole (of Life) as viewed by your personal lens. So when we look at an entire Life ,what must necessarily be components of this gift called Life. Obviously one looks at both personal and business dimensions in addition to social needs and health concerns. So, assuming you have sat and made a master plan on January 1 of every year encompassing all your goals and are earnestly watching your progress in each compartment and in overall terms, you are now one step ahead of everyone else in realizing your definition of your Personal Life and your understanding of the strategizing process.

Your life strategy defines your purpose in Life, you role as you view it in the world and your every special goals and plans to achieve your definition of well being. So assuming again that you are very clear with your life expectations and able to look at different aspects of your Life as one big bundle of joy and challenge, you now get close to seeing your Life Portfolio. Since Life is so personal and the things which you turn you on and give meaning to your Life maybe quite different than someone else, viewing and positioning your portfolio is important. You now get to the next step of self actualizing this portfolio.

A sample Life portfolio may see the incorporation of your personal goals in terms of health and relationships and where you would like to live/continue to live and a separate and special chapter on your very special relationships with your near and dear ones. It could also separately list your personal investment, retirement and vacation goals for the year and clarify your social and community interests.

To assist you in the fulfillment of your Life portfolio, positive thinking leads the way. Because a positive thought lifestyle and attitude allows you to only focus on the worthwhile and definite accomplishments, which are desirable within your Life portfolio. The greater your positive focus, the easier it will be for you to achieve your goals of personal happiness, wealth and superlative relationships. Since positive thinking does not exist in a vacuum, its constant focus on specific areas of your Life plan will help you focus your mental, emotional and spiritual powers in those areas of interest, thereby creating a faster level of success for you and all in your very special Life circle.

## POSITIVISM AND SELF-MOTIVATION

Self-motivation is the ultimate way of getting you from point A to point B with the least amount of strife and confusion. Self-motivation is a personal system you create to guide and move you in the direction of your dreams and wishes. If you have not yet taken the time to crystallize your goals and set a deadline to achieve them, then now is the best time to do it. Because without goals, all kinds of self- motivation will be useless and ineffective. It is like someone saying, "I want to get rich without defining what I understand as my very own personal definition of wealth." Without a precise and crystallized goal of what it means to be rich nothing can work to helping you get what you want.

So, what is self-motivation? It is taking responsibility for your Life. It is being mindful of what goals you set for yourself. You need to understand and realize that whatever you choose to think of becomes reality in your Life sooner or later. Therefore the power of your thought must never be forgotten. Because strong thoughts and feelings can transform a Life, either positively or negatively. Self-motivation is a constant process of encouragement, enthusiasm and self direction which you apply in as many waking hours as you can to guide you towards your dream. The most successful achievers in the world in any field, have always used the poser of self motivation to be more effective and make a greater difference in the world around them.

What role does Positivism play in this process? Very simple, constant and never ending positive spirit needs to be combined with your self-motivation process to move you towards your goal with increased velocity. Positive spirit encompasses, positive visualization, prayer, accompanied with focused thought in alignment with your goal ——----- constant awareness, belief and faith is your Power to reach your coveted point in Life. A combination of constant Positive Powers accompanied with self-motivation gets you faster to where you want to go and does this in a happy and successful way.

## POSITIVISM AND SELF CONCEPT

An understanding of what constitutes your self concept involves taking a mysterious journey into yourself. As you spend quality time with yourself researching and investigating your thoughts, feelings and value systems, you note that a lot of your thinking and values are shaped by others. Ever since childhood, parents and your immediate social and cultural system have taught you to believe that certain things are good or bad and we have rather subconsciously imbibed these values into our daily life. These thoughts, feelings and opinions now define the way we look at things and in a sense create an internal psychological mold. Such acquired values may not all hold themselves in good stead as you grow up. In fact, some of these values could be so negative that it may prevent you from reaching your goals.

Let me provide an example. If you are born in a poor family, where your parents have always made you feel that you will be nothing but poor all Life long then if you endeavor to get rich as you grow to maturity, such negative values may become a strong inhibitor to your personal success. So you need to first understand all your self concepts. A self concept is defined as the myriad of observations, experiences and feelings, which define how you feel about yourself. A self concept is a composite image of how you see yourself.

To make a dramatic shift in your self concept takes a lot of courage. You need to first be strong and objective enough to list and understand all the your traits, qualities and values, which make you define what you think of yourself. You then need to throw out all negative values, assumptions and feelings about your inadequacies, whether imagined or real. You then replace these negative values with positive ones. This is easily said but often is the most difficult thing to do for most people. It is however worth a try, since your Life is very valuable and you owe it to yourself to not only examine your weak points and assumptions but to try to make a positive change. Unless you are aware of these weak centers, making a positive change will be very difficult.

What is the role of positive thinking in its relationship with self concept? Believe me you need the strength and faith, which accompanies positive thinking to make a quantum change in your Life. You need to believe you deserve a better station in life and that there is never ending hope of progress as you work towards the achievement of your dream. Positive thinking constantly reminds you that your self concept could be limiting your true potential----- it assists in both identifying your negative values, attitudes and behavior and then helps you make a modification of some of these behavioral patterns---- you now enter a realm where you can look at things differently as you endeavor to change your Life.

In addition, an examination of your self concept could isolate several acquired strengths and tendencies. These strengths when isolated, channelized and focused could play an important role in the fulfillment of your dreams and goals. So, one must accentuate your strengths and negate your weaknesses and develop additional qualities which may be required in your quest to be the very best you can be.

Understanding all components which make up your me, your combined set of experiences which define who you see yourself as now and the subsequent elimination of weaknesses with accentuation of strengths combined with adding new talents, skills, visualizations, thoughts and effort will help you reach your goal faster and with much happiness and harmony.

# POSITIVISM AND SELF-IMAGE

Now that we have understand what self concept is, let us talk a little bit about your view on self image. Self image may be broadly defined as the sum of experiences which define who YOU think you are, as viewed from an external lens. This external lens, is the view point of the world as such world forms its opinion on your character, behavior and actions in the world. As you grow and develop you notice that certain behaviors, qualities and attitudes are accepted and admired by others and several other actions and behaviors are frowned upon by society and friends, in general. It is a normal tendency of all humans to be pleasing to others and in so many instances other people's values and definitions of how you must behave and act become your way of doing things. You may even compromise some of your values and attitudes to make others feel more happy. This behavior modification happens not only in external opinions forced on you by your environment but also sometimes by the ones most dear to you as your family, spouse and other loved ones, who criticize you in order to shape you according to their image of who they wish you to become.

So we now have a conflict in progress. You are a natural, god endowed human with your own unique set of traits and values. As you express yourself in society and in relationships you encounter resistance in the form of negative criticism and behavior from others, who do not approve of your behavior. So what does a human do in this situation? If the extent of the relationship is very deep and meaningful, it results in one modifying one's behavior and in the extreme case your character to keep someone else happy. In many instances, it could be the fear of being isolated and/or abandoned by a loved one if you do not engage in behavior modification. So your self concept, which is the way you naturally see yourself undisturbed by others views, can now be modified by your self image, which is a forced behavioral change to satisfy the perceived needs of a loved one. How does this affect you from a broader point of view? You could now be adopting a change in thoughts, feelings and actions which could go against the fulfillment of your dream and long term goal.

So how is one to make a change in this reality? Firstly by being honest with yourself and listing on the left side of a plain sheet of paper, all your acquired and self-trusted strengths and weaknesses and then on the other side of the page listing all your behavioral strength and weaknesses originating from your self image. If a loved one is involved getting them to do a parallel self concept and self image exercise would help. Then you need to get your loved one on board with what you are trying to accomplish and this throws up the challenge of having to sell the other person to buy into what may cause an obstruction in fulfillment of your long term goal.

If your partner sees this and realized that the end goal is for the fulfillment of both partner's common needs, this may create a motivation for the other person to allow you to develop your life plan in a way which creates the right environment for success.

Self actualization is the ultimate point in the Maslowian needs pyramid. As the psychologist Maslow indicated in his presentation of a pyramid of human needs, humans try to meet with their most urgent needs pictured at the base of the pyramid and then try to progressively move upwards to meet other important needs. The basal pyramid needs were the need for food and shelter. Then one progresses upwards to fulfill needs for acceptance from others and then further up the pyramid the need to be loved. The ultimate pinnacle of the pyramid was a person who has not only fulfilled his basal needs but is now self fulfilled in all perceived areas of his Life. He has organized his food and shelter needs and is accepted and loved by others in addition to having his ego needs met----he is now the co-creator of a a Life in tandem with what he truly wishes and desires.

Self actualization means that you have taken the time and trouble to understand yourself at all levels starting with your self concept and then proceeding towards an analysis and understanding of your self image. A person is truly blessed and advanced if he can get the world(self image) to see him just the way he sees and wants to be seen himself(self concept).Here is a human not afraid to take risks and bold enough to leave his footprint in the world. And this is ideally a human who does this with the utmost courage and faith and without stepping on others toes.

Positive thinking plays a clear role in focusing awareness of all the conscious and subconscious acquired traits----- which are influenced by other people, situations and circumstances in your life. Positive thinking teaches you to first understand these influences and then negate the worthless influences, which hold you back. Positive thinking now becomes a beacon in the journey from negative self image to positive self concept and leads you to greatness and success.

# POSITIVISM AND THE LAW OF ATTRACTION

The Law of Attraction basically postulates that you can get anything you wish if you truly believe in a specific set of goals and truly believe you deserve the end result. And combined with faith and confidence in a universal energy,which assists to get to where they want to go, combined with a visualization of achievement of the end result, will always get you where you want to go.

What role does Positivism play in your journey utilizing the Law of Attraction? Very simply, positivism assists in the quick achievement of your dream employing principles of Law of Attraction. What happens to most dream-makers is that they initially focus on a goal but soon lose their focus. The Law of Attraction works best in an environment where there is constant focus and reinforcement of the principles underlying principle. What are these underlying principles?

They are in no particular order of importance, but are listed as follows:

1.  The ability to focus on your end goal.

2.  To ability to clearly visualize attainment of the goal before its manifestation.

3.  To ability to use the principles behind the law of intention.

4.  The power to be strong and persistent as you face headwinds in your journey towards accomplishment of your goal.

5.  To believe you deserve what you intend.

6.  To keep moving fearlessly in the direction of your dream, irrespective of how strong the obstacles are.

7.  To believe in yourself, and in the fact that your self concept always rules over self image.

Positive thinking helps in each of these seven critical areas in terms of successful completion and achievement of your dream. It does this as follows:

1.      Positivism allows you keep focusing on your end goal by utilizing the principle of constant concentration.

2.      Positivism provides the reinforcement to gibe you permission to visualize achievement of your goal and how that makes you feel prior to the actual manifestation of the result.

3.      Positivism helps you believe in the power of intending your results. Simply you use positive thinking to send out your power of intention which results in speedy achievement of your goal.

4.      Positivism helps you stay on course with great determination as you face strong headwinds preventing you from quickly achieving your dream.

5.      Positive thinking along with constant affirmation allows you to believe that you truly deserve what you wish.

6.      Strong and constant positive thought develops the strength and persistence to get to where you want to go in spite of innumerable difficulties on your life course.

7.      By constantly associating positivism with your self concept, which involves an inherent belief in yourself, your abilities, qualities and dreams. It becomes easier to forge ahead, focusing more on your self concept an compared to your self image, which is how others view you now.

These seven applications must be read in conjunction with the seven principles of the law of attraction So 1 outlined under law of attraction works with 1 underlined in applications of positive thinking to the law of attraction.


Nothing operates in a vacuum. And therefore positive thinking, to have its greatest impact, must work in relationship with specific principles. This chapter is intended to demonstrate application of positive thinking in different Life situations. Application of positive thinking to the principles of the law of attraction, make success that much easier and sweeter.

## POSITIVISM AND THE ENERGY OF DESIRE

Desire is the fabric of motivation. Without a burning desire guiding you into a specific direction nothing great gets accomplished in the World. If you do not have a burning desire to achieve anything you must question what is topping this drive. Because without a way of channeling the desire all the laws and positivism will not help you lead a richer and happier life.

Now, assuming you are an energetic person full of desire to live your life to the fullest, how do you channel this desire with positivism to get what you want. You first must understand that accentuated positivism is a companion to strong desire and if you have these two qualities you are on your way to great success. Energy and Positive desire are great burning forces which move you at an exponential level from point a to point b.

Desire must be channeled by constant repetition of the purpose of desire. This channeling is done by using positive thoughts to focus on all your desires and then allowing the law of attraction to take over and help you accomplish your dreams.

Life is all about good relationships. The main types of relationships are as follows;

1.  *Relationships with family and loves ones.*

2.  *Relationships with society at large.*

3.  *Relationships with your ideas and emotions.*

4.  *Relationships with the external Life environment you operate in.*

5.  *Relationships with nature.*

The truly successful people employ optimum relationships t all these five levels. Positivism is the beacon of light which help0s people be and stay happy---- it assists them in achieving good relationships at all levels of their life. By applying positivism with the thought that people are good and the projection that good things will ice your way if you treat others well and work honestly and with complete desire, determination and focus will create a better life for you and for everything and everyone you touch.

Health is truly a divine gift. In North America there is too much emphasis provided to the physical form. Billions of dollars get spent on fulfilling your physical cravings, while at the other extreme you find physical fitness buffs using the latest trainer and diet menu to aftertaste restrengthen and beautify their bodies. What is unknown o to all these avid pursuers of physical gratification and/or physical beauty, that health is not a physical affair exclusively.

Health is a total energy reflection of an individual. As such it encompasses all levels of human relationship and interaction. A truly health person is healthy from the inside out. What I mean is that one needs to work on ones inner improvement and development in terms of understanding him sled and his relationship to the world at large.   He needs to understand that he has to work on being happy and mentally and emotionally fulfilled in addition to pursing physical fitness goals. He needs to find the right balance few himself of his physical, mental, emotional and spiritual needs to really be health.

Positivism allows the individual to focus and accentuate all levels of his Life encompassing his physical, mental, emotional and spiritual directions and leanings. Positivism helps identify lacunae in his development and through meditation assists in balancing diverse needs and requirements of all different aspects of his personality.

True health is a sparkling, effervescent energy. It is a feeling of boundless happiness and care for others. *T is a feeling of complete energy around your life. Good health assisted with positive application and awareness creates a good, caring and successful persons one who helps others and is helped by the universal energy around him for all good must be s paid back in kind, sooner or later.*

Longevity and a disease free life are not only dependent on genetic factors. They are also critically influenced by your attitude towards life, the quality of your relationships and how you feel about yourself. There is an intrinsic connection between emotions and the physical organism. This connection has been proved innumerably in scientific journals. Psychosomatics is a study of how the state of mind, including emotional state affect the functioning, vitality and life of the physical organism.

It follows that positive thinking is the elixir of a life filled with great physical energy and good health. It is obvious that high physical energy and great health stem the tide of disease. Positivism can now come to the aid of anyone who applies it religiously to improve and enhance his Life and accentuates longevity

## POSITIVISM AND WEALTH CREATION AND MAINTENANCE

Wealth creation is a function of positive goal setting an an undying determination to get what you want in the fastest possible time. The qualities and skills that it takes to attract and hold on to wealth are numerous. However, it is very rare that a wealthy person can hold on to his wealth indefinitely. There are rough economic patches, especially for the entrepreneur who stakes his life, talent and energy in pursing a unique business dream. However r, it is always the tortoise who wins the long term wealth creation race and not the hare, who is known to shoot in quick outbursts only to get fatigues as the race prolongs itself.

Positivism helps you believe in yourself. It helps you constantly stroke yourself as you attempt to scale higher heights of financial success. And it helps you stay the course when things get tough. Positivism is a must addition to the wealth creation and maintenance process.

Stress is a common affliction in the Western world. As Life gets faster, the pressure to keep up with it increases. Not everyone can perform at a superlative pace, and this is where positivism assists in raising the bar for an average performer. Stress is a classic fight or fly response where an individual either faces up to a new challenge or runs away from it.

This response mechanism was learn from our ancestors and is typical of their reaction when they faced a formidable beast in their hunting fields; they had to choose rather quickly to either fight and vanquish it or run away from the scary animal.

Positivism allows you to hold your course. It assists you in facing your Life problems squarely and courageously never flinching from your established and written purposes. Positivism becomes a light in the darkness, which when properly understood can assist in overcoming your stress issues and creating a more balanced person---- a person who can operate in a challenging, uncertain and volatile world and yet have the power, strength and purpose to gain what he wishes.

## POSITIVISM AND ENTREPRENEURSHIP

Entrepreneurship is one of the last bastions of   free enterprise. In a developed country like the US, the only real opportunity available for substantial capital accumulation is through creation of a successful business. And entrepreneurship represents one of the most challenging fields in human existence. You take a risk and put everything on the line-----your money, your credit, your relationships. You are in search of a big dream, a dream which can make you rich beyond imagination. However, till you reach a point of financial and business success, you are working in the dark. An individual needs great courage, vision and persistence to succeed in business. And he needs to muster all the strength he can as he takes on this life size challenge.

Positivism keeps the flow of energy moving in the direction of a dream. Positivism strokes you and make you believe you will succeed. It gives you the motivation to dream big, to act big and to achieve a goal far beyond most peoples imagination. Positivism thus becomes a contributing force in the entrepreneurship effort to become rich and financially independent.

## POSITIVISM AND TIME MANAGEMENT

Time management is a much needed art in this day and age. With distractions, advertisements and social media hounding us every second of the day, it becomes so important to phase out all the background noise and focus your time on what is most important to you----- the achievement of your very own private goals. It is now that time management starts playing a very important role. When you stop and look at your Life, what do you really own, in terms of resources, to get what you want? Time, energy and money. For most people starting their road to success, money is a initial limiting factor. But energy to dream big and the courage to transform that dream into a reality in real time is what matters most. If time and energy are all you have to reach the pinnacle of success, then is not the organization and planning/management of time important in getting to where you want to go? And yet this is what most people do ineffectively. I see poor time management utilization at all levels of society and across all cross sections of the population. Most unfortunately, this is something not taught in our schools and universities alike.

Positivism helps you to focus on what is most essential for the achievement of your life goals. It helps you first list the important skills, education and networks you need to succeed and then helps you stay in focus to draw a time management plan which gives maximum attention to development of these resources and attributes.

# POSITIVISM AND THE ART OF ALLOWING

The art of allowing is basically a mental process which allows you to get what you want. Societies and cultures do not normally support a big dream. It almost always comes that Society, in general, supports a performance at the common denominator of your social and business circle. People tend to approximate performance of their natural or acquired social and inherited family group. In order for you to be super successful you need to step out of this comfort zone of past conditioning and dare to stand alone. In the process you will meet a lot of conscious and subconscious resistance from your peer group.

The Art of Allowing is synonymous with the Art of Intention. Very simply, you intend your future results. You allow yourself mentally, emotionally and spiritually to receive the fruits of your efforts. And this allowing and intention happens right at the beginning of your Life trip---- you intend to be successful, you allow all good things to pass and all positive energy to be attracted into your life to get you where you want to get in a happy, quick and easy manner.

Positivism is the motivating force, which allows you to receive blessings and positive energy in advance. Positive thinking allows you to become different from your peers----- it creates the right environment for the law of intention to work a miracle in your life.

# POSITIVISM AND PARENTING

Parents play a super important role in the early psychological molding of their children. In so many instances, poor parents beget poor children and talented parents create geniuses in their children But this is not necessarily the rule to be followed. America is full of examples where impoverished and disadvantaged children have risen above their bad family conditioning to mark a place in the sun. If you realize your important role as a parent, then you will take care to create a very positive environment for your children. You will go out of your way to encourage then to be and do better--- you will give them greater faith and confidence in their talents, and provided them with the inspiration to aspire to be the business, social and community leaders of tomorrow.

Positivism in a real parent child situation creates and transfers this positive attitude to children. Children are very curious by nature and imbibe the values projected in their surroundings by parents and friends alike. Would it be not a great gift to give the gift of positivism to your children. Now parenting can work with positivism to make it easier for children to face the world and assist these young precious ones to carve their own special and unique place in it.

# POSITIVISM AND THE POWER OF THE MASTER MIND

What is the Master Mind? The Master Mind Principle is an energy force created as a result of combined mental, emotional and spiritual energies of a group of like minded motivated people. A true master mind can create massive personal and financial results. Have you ever tried to organize regular meetings around a group of similar minded people who work together in a common direction?

Positivism, when used in the Master Mind group amplifies the effect of this approach. You now reach a situation where you can be ten, twenty or one hundred times more effective by combining the positive energy and purpose of a group of individuals. Why not try this experiment yourself and you will be astonished with the results forthcoming.

The Law of Karma has a huge following and belief in spiritually inclined countries in the East. India and China come to mind at the outset. The Law of Karma says there is a cause and effect relationship to everyone's life. This Law goes beyond the scientific explanation of cause end effect as propounded by renowned scientist, Newton. The law and effect in Hindu philosophy has to do with causal relationships between different lifetimes. This Karmic connection puts forth the notion and belief that this is not our first or last life on earth Whether you choose to agree with this thinking or not is irrelevant. What is more important is an understanding of how our actions can create massive positive or negative effects in our future. And this has not only do with our actions but also our thoughts and feelings towards others.

Positivism tries to reverse the negative effects of poor Karmic thoughts, feelings and actions towards others. By staying positive with a constant approach to helping others in whatever you do, you start reversing the negative cycle of anger, depression and fault finding. Positivism now becomes a beacon of light which helps you not only help yourself but also others with your new found energy.

# SECTION 4

*-APPLICATION OF POSITIVE PRINCIPLES IN CREATING HAPPINESS*

PAGE LEFT INTENTIONALLY BLANK

CHAPTER 19

POSITIVISM AND HAPPINESS

## Definition of Happiness

Happiness is the most wonderful and endearing human experience. It lights up your Life and Soul. It brings forth a gust of positive energy---- a radiance that touch everyone who comes in close contact with you. It is felt even if you do not communicate verbally with someone. It is truly something everyone aspires to, consciously or subconsciously.

How can you define something as beautiful, intangible and esoteric as happiness? Books have been written, quite unsuccessfully about it. Movies depict its magic. Songs we hear all day talk about the mystery of happiness acquired through personal love relationships. Poets extol the virtues and ideals of true happiness. And world religions all profess to have the magic key which will unlock the kingdom of happiness. But yet no one is close enough to attract and hold happiness permanently. This is most unfortunately the human condition. Although we try so hard to hold on to happiness, it slips between our fingers. We are offered brief glimpses of happiness in fleeting relationships and in quiet moments, but cannot hold on to this mysterious magic. So how can one define the undefinable? How can one grasp the mysterious bounty of fullness associated with happiness? I can only humbly offer my version of happiness.

For one thing, happiness is not a thought. It is a wonderful, beautiful feeling. It is being in a space with no boundaries. It is living in a sparkling effervescent condition. It is a space which is permeated by not only positive feelings but with a mysterious contact with perfect relationship with everything around you. It is a contact unconditionally in total sync to with all situations and conditions in your inner environment and outer one.

So why are we talking about happiness in a essay on positivism? Because positivism is the first step which can take you towards unbounded love and happiness. Without this first step there is no movement towards this unbounded happiness. Since we all need and deserve happiness, does it not make sense to discuss the intimate relationship between positivism and happiness? To me, it does. It is the only way---- the only key to a different life than the one we experience daily, which is a life of stress, anxiety and much confusion.

But this is a better way to live. It is not a way to escape from your environment or responsibilities but merely a fresh and new way of looking at your relationships and reactions to your external and internal environment. This is why the final section of this book deals with happiness and propounds the fact, in no uncertain terms, that everything else we are trying to do leads up to the mastery and acquisition of happiness. Please note that this acquisition is not one which we are used to in terms of owning and possessing something like a car, a house, a woman or a child. Happiness cannot be possessed or permanently acquired through any technique. All you can do is keep the window open and invite the fresh air of happiness to grace your Life. If you can do this you are doing more to live a better, more happy life than 99.99% of the population. And if this book helps you even just accomplish this, it has served its purpose quintessentially.

*Because happiness is all that matters……………*

# CHAPTER 20

## RELATIONSHIP BETWEEN POSITIVE THINKING AND HAPPINESS

Positive thinking leads the way to happiness. Imagine positive thinking as a gateway. An opening, which leads you to an opportunity of happiness. Please note I mention an opportunity to a life of happiness. Positive thinking, like most other things in life, does not guarantee a future filled with happiness. It just provides a greater probability of achieving and holding on to happiness.

How does positive thinking work in this way? By negating thoughts and feelings related to inadequacy, depression, self deprecation and negative conditioning---- all factors discussed earlier in this book. Positive thinking creates and environment to attract an unknown essence into your Life. Now this all sounds too philosophical and esoteric? Since happiness is such a personal experience and this experience has different interpretations and opinions, all that matters is how you feel deep within yourself. If you feel that magic enter your life--- a magic of inner harmony, peace and love you know you are on the right track; if not, then the challenge is for you to do more inner exploration and self study to coordinate the value of positive thinking with your most important need to be happy and satisfied with yourself and the world around you.

Once the mind is exalted to a higher energy stage through positive thinking and negative experiences and feelings are deprecated, you open up a vast space of possibility. This vast space is not only related to achievement of your worldly goals but also more importantly, the opening up of your inner spiritual center, where you have an opportunity to really understand and feel yourself. This is truly an individual and private experience. It seems so important to find ourselves in all ways and not only in traditional cultural ways. We all have a living connection with the Unknown and Divine force and part of your effort should necessarily be devoted to understanding and connecting to this Super Energy source.

Intuition, the divine manifestation of inner contact can then guide you to doing what is best for you in any given situation and crisis, helping you to overcome your obstacles and achieve both your outer worldly goals, which now provides you a glimpse of your inner beauty and magic.

It is impossible to be happy and negative. What is negative thinking? It is a destructive force which creeps into our moments and life suddenly and sometimes without any advance warning. Fear and desire are instances of how negativism can creep into your thoughts and feelings. Fear of insecurity, of not having enough of what you want and need, fear of not being loved, fear of not being accepted by our peer group, family and society are some of the reasons which draw negative feelings into our Life. Desire can also have a similar effect. When desire is fulfilled and pleasure realized, we appear to be very satisfied.

However, when desire gets thwarted and unrealized then there is a fear of loss of something we deeply want and this too can cause negativism. Once a person succumbs to negativism, it draws other bad things in your life, like depression and anxiety and in extreme cases,, alcoholism and drug abuse.

The only way to lick the problems caused by negativism is through conscious vigilance. This is easier than it sounds. The price for inner growth is eternal awareness. Once you are consciously aware of negative thoughts, the very awareness has the power to permanently vanquish that negative thought and feeling, giving you an opportunity to move into the positive zone. The more you stay in the positive Zone, the closer you get to realization of both your written goals and dreams and your contact with the Universal force, which is the only medium for attraction of that mysterious energy and love called Happiness.

*And is that not the ultimate purpose of human existence? Being happy all the time and empowering others to find happiness with dignity and peace.*

# CHAPTER 21

## NEGATION OF POSITIVISM

It appears in the Western world that most success is judged by material success. Since times immemorial, the cultural connotation for happiness is going to school, getting educated, finding a good job, finding a good mate, procreating a family and living happily ever after. We have now found that this social model does not stand the test of time---- testament to this fact is the 50 per cent divorce rate in North America. Surely there must be a better and easier way to find happiness.

If one stops just craving for more, if one can stop the never ending desire for more and more stuff, then one has a chance to discover a quiet, inner opening----- this now becomes an invitation to enter a new inner world blessed with much peace and happiness. This does not mean that you kill your desire for better material things---- it just means you put this in its place and perspective. You do not allocate all your available energy to the acquisition of money, sex, power and social standing but instead devote some energy to other valuable pursuits, like charitable causes and the spiritual search for a better you.

Negation of positivism occurs when you get so preoccupied with desire fulfillment that you miss the real purpose of life. By a never ending search for more and material goods, you invite negativism. This creeps in when you cannot get something you wish or feel you need. Fulfillment of your material needs and desires invites gratification---- loss or non attainment of some of these desires results in a feeling of worry, tension and negativism. In a sense, you negate positivism by such incessant action.

Positivism can be the first step to disassociate and detach yourself from the numerous demands placed on your time and life by others. You need to free yourself from the clutches of desire. Allocate some time to quietness and meditation and try to see the bigger picture. Positivism is the first door, which when opened provides a possibility to a more fulfilled and happy Life.

# CHAPTER 22

## POSITIVISM, HAPPINESS AND KARMA

Karma is a strong force. In Hindu religion, which believes in reincarnation of the soul, Karma is the price you pay in this Life for the good or bad deeds you performed in your last life. Whether this is true or not is irrelevant-------what is important to understand is that we are all born different and unequal. We are unequal in the sense that some of us are born in wealthy families and allowed opportunity to study and have an opportunity to enjoy a good economic life while others are born to poverty in limited opportunity family environments. This does not mean or imply that the ones who are born unequal cannot surpass the more equal. American history points to numerous individuals, who have surpassed the negative values of their environment and reached positions of great power and privilege. What I am trying to expand on is the fact that different individuals have different mental and emotional capacities. Some can withstand a lot of stress, others cannot. Some are very healthy while others have poor health.

The real challenge in gaining happiness is to negate the bad effects of your special Karma. With positivism and good expectation accompanied with strong self faith and belief, you can turn around the corner and beat a bad situation. The strength can be acquired through using some of the principles of positive thinking mentioned in this publication. I would still encourage you to read other classics in Positive thinking--- these are mentioned in the suggested bibliography appearing at the end of this book. By opening your life and Karma to new possibilities with effective use of Positive thinking and a strong faith in the assistance you can receive from Universal Energy, you can achieve both material and inner prosperity. Positivism conquers not only your bad Karma but also creates an invitation to a more happier and fulfilled Life.

# CHAPTER 23

## THE SHADOW OF FEAR-THE ANTITHESIS OF HAPPINESS

Fear needs to be understood if you are to have a fighting chance to acquire a lasting and deep peace in your Life. And the conquest of fear is truly challenging. It is so hard to quantify the origins of fear. But there are two kinds of fear: one justified natural fear, which comes when you face a poisonous snake on your way home and secondly, the unjustified imagined fear, which we deal with every day when we imagine something nasty may happen to us. This second fear disturbs completely our inner and outer peace.

Meditation is the most effective way of discovering the origin of fear. Only with a quite mind, which is now undistributed by the constant bombardment of messages from the external world with all its never ending demands can one open up the inner space to understand and deal with fear. As long as there is a shadow of fear lingering in our background, it is hard to bring in the perfume of happiness.

Learn to deal with your fear, learn to be aware of the negativism ---- now make a determined effort to step out of this self imposed cage to a better and more prosperous and happy Life.

# CHAPTER 24

## POSITIVISM AND THE CONQUER OF ANGER AND WORRY

Anger and worry are two demons we face on a daily basis. And both these emotions are highly destructive and negative. Anger expresses itself in all kinds of relationships with loved ones and strangers alike, when one feels his road to prosperity and fulfillment thwarted------- whether this obstruction is due to lack of money, lack of a job, poor health or other reasons. The anger ushers outwards to destroy other valuable relationships.

Worry also acts as a negative accelerator-------- worry is very much connected with fear. If you fear something bad may happen to you, you now trigger the worry feeling. This extremely negative emotion may cause depression, and in extreme cased lead to suicide, alcoholism and/or drug abuse.

There is no simple way to face anger and worry other than accepting that this is really happening to you at a certain point of time in your Life. Do note this is happening in relationship- with some idea or feeling you have in terms of a visualization of something bad which may happen to you----- you are now projecting negatively on a possible effect of some action you are undertaking now, an action of whose effect you are not certain. Positive thinking and non stop awareness are the only effective ways to conquer worry and anger. The mere watching of the anger and/or worry, if properly done can create a new space for you----- one where you do not accept the worry or anger and let it goal. Just release the worry and anger and pray for a more positive peace to come to your Life. Happiness is your birthright and will be attracted to you as long as you can be detached towards your feelings of inadequacy, anger and worry.

# CHAPTER 25

## SUMMARY

This book is a journey into the discovery of positive thinking. Unlike many books on this subject, which hype the word, positive thinking, this book goes into an intensive process of understanding how to apply Positive thinking in your Life. As the proof of the pudding is in the eating, the value of any book on Positive thinking is in its ability to transform your Life. And this is what the author attempts to do with this publication.

The book starts with a reason why one should consider employing Positive thinking in his Life. It then discusses the four major Laws: the Law of Attraction, the Law of success, the Law of Sub-conscious power and the Law of Psycho-cybernetics. These four laws represent the major pillars on which the philosophy and application of Positive Thinking rests.

The book then discusses positive thinking in live relationships. It is quick to point out that positive thinking does not exist in a vacuum but in relationship to other thoughts, ideas and feelings, which create building blocks towards a better and more happier life.

And finally, the book discusses the relationship between Positivism and Happiness. Deep down we aspire to enjoy a life blessed with much happiness and peace. But this becomes an elusive dream for many. Positivism prepares the way for one to experience a true and lasting happiness.

# CHAPTER 26

## CONCLUSION

We are blessed with the precious gift of Life. But many of us take this gift for granted. Instead of trying to really uplift oneself to a higher station, we get dragged down by our past conditioning and false preconceived notions of living. This results in much negativism, pain and despair.

We truly deserve a better way of living---- one in which we can achieve our dreams while contributing positively to the well-being of others. Positivism is the first step which assists you in starting your journey back home. An understanding of the four basic laws, combined with knowledge of how positive thinking operates through your Life relationships assists the reader in re-looking his way of Existence. By introducing and maintaining positivism, which naturally involve the negation of disturbing and worrying thoughts and feelings, one starts this journey into oneself.

Positive thinking is available to everyone, rich and poor alike to improve their life. May this book be a beginning in your eternal quest to find yourself and to create true meaning and purpose in your Life. May this book help accelerate your progress into a  Life filled with much love, blessings and kindness. The author prays for your continued development. All things are possible if you dare to pray and believe in yourself. Positive thinking really works. Give it a shot and see how it transforms your Life into a beautiful, lively and enduring experience…………………………………..

## SUGGESTED BIBLIOGRAPHY/FURTHER READING

1. Think and Grow Rich by Napoleon Hill.

2. Psycho-Cybernetics by Maxwell Maltz.

3. The Law of Attraction, Basics of the teachings of Abraham by Gerry and Esther Hicks.

4. The Power of your Sub-Conscious Mind by Joseph Murphy.

5. The Prosperity Bible by Napoleon Hill.

6. The Law of Positive thinking, A success guide for teens and young adults—Raj D. Rajpal (createspace.com and amazon.com)

7. You have it all-your Life is yours to truly discover and enjoy by Raj D. Rajpal(createspace.com and amazon.com)

8. Success through a Positive Mental Attitude-Napoleon Hill and Clement Stone.

THIS PAGE IS LEFT INTENTIONALLY BLANK

THIS PAGE LEFT INTENTIONALLY BLANK

Raj D. Rajpal has spent his lifetime serving and educating others. After operating a financial planning and risk management practice in Toronto, Canada for around twenty years, he felt his knowledge, education and skills would continue to be served profitably through an education and consulting practice. Several years later, a publishing company, Pioneer Communication was born. This company was the primary vehicle for dissemination of Raj's teachings.

Raj has written over twelve books. His two latest books on personal development are both on Positive Thinking. The first book is entitled, Positive Thinking for Teenagers and Young Adults and this book is entitled Positive Power.

A lot of the ideas in this book are based on real experiences and lifetime applications and teachings of Raj. The ideas originate from ancient laws, like the Law of Attraction, the Law of Success, the Law of Psycho-Cybernetics and the Law of the Sub-Conscious Mind, among others.

Raj holds a GCE-O level degree from the University of Cambridge, U.K. Raj also holds a Masters Degree in Business Administration from the University of Dayton, Ohio. He has taught and trained sales counselors and is also a public and motivational speaker.

Numerous education and industry awards earned by Raj include a Public Speaking Trophy, instructor status in the Larry Wilson Counselor Selling Program, USA and Provisional Membership in the Million Dollar Round table, USA. Raj is also a Canadian National Quality Award winner and Magna cum laude graduate from the MBA Program at the University of Dayton, Ohio. He has completed the Bob Proctor Series 1 and Series 2 programs on Advanced Motivation.

*www.thepioneercommunication.com*